jackknife

PITT POETRY

50 YEARS

SERIES

Ed Ochester, Editor

jackknife

new and selected poems

jan beatty

UNIVERSITY OF PITTSBURGH PRESS

Published by the University of Pittsburgh Press, Pittsburgh, Pa., 15260
Copyright © 2017, Jan Beatty
All rights reserved
Manufactured in the United States of America
Printed on acid-free paper
10 9 8 7 6 5 4 3 2 1

ISBN 13: 978-0-8229-6449-0
ISBN 10: 0-8229-6449-X

Cover art: Andy Warhol, *Knives*, 1981. Image and artwork © 2016 The Andy Warhol
Foundation for the Visual Arts, Inc. / Artists Rights Society (ARS), New York

Cover design by Joel W. Coggins

for women everywhere
who are told to be nice
and to shut up—

contents

New Poems

1.

2.

from Mad River

from Boneshaker

from Red Sugar

from The Switching/Yard

new poems

1

I watched the waitress for a thousand years
Saw a wheel inside a wheel, heard a call within a call
— Gillian Welch, I Dream a Highway

Inside the Cardinal

I'm in the belly of a bird and I'm singing red—
my sharp crest spiking when I down-slur.
I'm your mother's voice as she spots me
from the old porch, the shrill
of the stand-up Yamaha, the vibrating e-string
on the yellow strat—
Will you love my loud, metallic song?

I like to sit low in the shrubs,
and hang out in the woodlots.
Don't try to explain my sound—
it's too red, too
hot—
Look at me hunched over, my tail
pointed straight down.

It's just a small fire in me but soon
it will flame,
with the next intruder, the next shot
of wind, the next mourning:
filling the air with a dark carbon—
it will take your head off
a thousand times over.

Stricken

We're sitting in Uncle Sam's Subs, splitting
a cheesesteak, when Kat says:
I think I should buy a gun.
I look up at her puffy face, and she's staring,
her hands shaking. On medication for
schizophrenia, she's serious.
I say, *Tell me why you need a gun.*
Her voice getting louder: *You know why.*
No, no I don't, I say.
In case I need it. I might need it to shoot somebody.
I give her a hard look—*You don't need a gun.*
No one is after you.
She stares back: *You might be after me.*
I don't know what to say—I never know what to say.
I know it's not her speaking, but it's my friend,
far away in some other stricken mind.
What's it like to know you're right/
you're in danger—
and the world says no?
Every woman I know has lived that.
I say: *I would never hurt you. I'm not a threat to you.*
She laughs, says, *Well, you might be.*
The laughing scares me.
I want out of this place,
this sub shop, to walk away,
knowing she can't walk out of her mind, leave
the illness behind. The long minutes,
the long, long minutes. Kat says, *What do you think?*
I think we should eat our sandwiches, then
take a walk, I say.
What about the gun?

Let's talk about it later, I say,
not knowing a thing.
Not knowing a goddamn thing.

The Kindness

Banff, Alberta

The mother elk & 2 babies are sniffing
the metal handle of the bear-proof trash bin.
I remember the instructions for city people:
3 football fields of space between you &
the elk if their babies are with them.
I'm backing up slowly,
watching the calves run into each other
as they bend to eat grass/look up
at the mother at the same time.
The caramel color of their coat,
the sloping line of their small snouts &
I want to hold that beauty,
steal it for me,
but I'm only on football field #2 & backing
into the woods past the lodge pole pines.
Their fragility, their awkward bumping
opens me to a long ago time—

   a hand on the door,
   I was walking in
to the psych hospital in Pittsburgh,
feeling broken & stripped down—

   a hand on the door
   from around my body
& I looked up to see the body
of a man, who said:
Let me get that for you—

   a hand on the door
   & the bottom of me
   dropped/

I couldn't breathe for the kindness.
I couldn't say how deep that went
for me.
I had been backing up, awkward/
I had been blind to my own beauty.

The Secret Book and Record Store

On Wicklow Street in County Dublin,
the freaky doll heads sit next to the
books on how to please a woman, how
to cook explosives, and how to write a screenplay.
Dermott, the shaved-head black-
teeshirted proprietor with the heavy metal belt
talks about poetry and how
light could look like an approach to
a destination, or it could look like that
yellow-y light that lives outside a prison, giving
you that feeling of not breathing.
The narrow aisles are lined with brown
strongboxes of books, Guinness memorabilia,
political stickers and buttons.
Freebird Records are in the back, with all-vinyl
rock 'n 'roll, old punk and teeshirts with
pictures of Marley, Dylan and Clapton in a row.
The store's motto: "Abandon hope all ye who enter."
Now Dermott's talking about Kilmainham Prison:
When they built it, it had toilets, but then
they took them out, the prisoners were having too much fun.
His eyes sparkle and he leans in:
It's made of limestone, he says, which absorbs
water from the ground—so it stays freezing all the time.
Even so, during the famine, people
would commit crimes just to get in.
He said that just beyond the prison is an art gallery that's
quite nice—IMMA (Irish Museum of Modern Art)—
used to be an old soldier's rest home.
He's quieting down now, leaning back on
the wooden stool behind the old register:

One more thing he wants me to know:
that in poetry the light in the distance could be
the grand opening to a new heart—
or it could be the end of the line, like
the feeling of running out of light,
like the prison he knows,
Kilmainham.

Asylum

after Roselia Asylum and Maternity Hospital, corner of Cliff and Manilla

This is the house I was born in.

Look at it. Asylum.

Narrate it:

Notice the sloping cornice, look at the curved windows, etc.

This is the house I was born in.

The cast-iron balconies/not wide enough for bodies.

Look at the photos:

3 stories, 8 front windows and a wide door.

Dark red brick/inlaid with brown stone.

Women's bodies/expelling/banishing/

Leaving the babies there.

Look at the photos, include the photos.

Abortion with Gun Barrel

The 12 year-old walks thin, like a child/
her hair alive in vibrating threads
in the clinic light.
Her mother: *My daughter. I give my permission.*
And the girl cannot be real, or the sky
would burn—not bleed like it does in
the waiting room of grown women.
The mother in the brittle inner office scribbles
her name small on the collapsing form.
Now move the flying hands of the counselor
who becomes the first bird,
stripping the sky blank with air leaving.
Now she walks back to the maze of illuminated
bodies to find a way to make herself dissolve:
Not what I wanted for you, not this.
In the inner body of the clinic, the divining
of this choice: the small name solid,
the songbird stopped/
the singing continues.
I am the counselor,
there are cracks in the barrel of the gun/
there is aiming/
shots of sorrow—
shots of light.
I am ruinous with light, we are ruinous with making
our lives in the procedure room.
The 12 year-old opens the leaving door—
a bird let loose, no clear note to sing.
Song of sorrow and praise as she wears
the skin of herself,
this idea of skin that she's learning.

The World between Jim Morrison's Legs

I'm standing on 18th & Speedway, looking up:
between the legs of god it's a red & white swirl
of paint, I'm inside his thickness & his I'm-already-
fucking-you look & on the oceanwalk the minor gods
assemble: Harold Perry singing & playing his
John Carruthers guitar, strapped
to his body: teeshirts for sale, a leather satchel
of CD's, 3-inch orange amp strapped
to his solar plexus for sound.
His black-turbaned afro/leather visor on top
adds a foot to his height.
He says: Look at them, they take
pictures like I'm a monkey.
The Japanese guy 5 ft away aims his cell,
a white middle-aged tourist in teeshirt runs up:
Can I ask you something?
Were you the one in the movie?
Yeah, says Harold, Point of No Return—
good gig, had lunch with Bridget Fonda,
ASCAP & the whole thing, still get money
from that. His green eyes laser the crowd, he
yells: I got S-4XXL. Buy a teeshirt. I got one
to fit even you, he calls to an overweight man
& his family passing. I'm the only one who's
got your size. The man looks stung/half smiles
& drops his eyes & Harold whips around
on his inline skates, smiling every time
he jams the whammy bar. Like it's coming
from another body, his clear voice lives far back
in his throat: infinite abundance, he says.
I shake his hand—then pull back.

I can hear Morrison's take on this:

> trop-ic cor-ri-dor
>
> trop-ic trea-sure
>
> what got us this far
>
> to this mild equator?

Between god's legs there are no answers—
if he could jack off right here on Speedway,
I know he would, but 3:15, 7/22/13, there's
an old guy in the alley peeing by the dumpster,
in full view of the Mojo King and everyone
else. A man in a yellow/green/red turban rolls by
with his cart yelling: Baby Reggae!
Itsy Bitsy Spider Reggae!
Right here!

Low-Rider

Nikki's in the kitchen of the artist residency,
talking about merkins.
What? I say.
You know, they're kind of like pussy wigs
made of faux fur, sort of like wearing earrings—
cute, but I'm not sure who wears them.
6 ½ months pregnant, she's jump-talking:
I think of my baby like it's an arm.
That's how liberal I am about it.
I don't know what she means, but
I find out that Kate Winslet wore one
when she filmed *The Reader*.
Kate tells *Allure*: *Because of years of waxing,*
as all of us girls know, it doesn't come back
quite the way it used to.
Nikki and I drive to the art gallery to see
Rose, the low-rider, painting her '69 Impala.
Rose, with her dusty boots and sideways cap
makes me stop thinking. Nikki keeps talking:
I can't see down there because I'm knocked up,
I usually trim it, but I can't have a relationship
with my parts right now.
I can tell Rose thinks we're a couple, that
the baby bump in Nikki's black dress is ours.
The Daily Beast says it's usually beaver pelts,
while men wear loops or chains, more
like a fur codpiece, and
everyone's wearing them:
Patricia Arquette in *Human Nature*,
Rooney Mara in *The Girl with the Dragon Tattoo*,
Samantha in *Sex and the City*.

The woman cadaver in *Boardwalk Empire*
keeping it real for the Prohibition era,
and I wonder, is the hair supposed to look dead, too?
I'm watching Rose, the spray painted Impala.
She says, *I had to rebuild the carburetor*
this morning, and I'm nodding,
Mary-Louise Parker in *Angels in America*,
Jake Gyllenhal in *Love and Other Drugs*,
Gretchen Mol (all skin) in *The Notorious Betti Page*,
but so many questions: what about industrial glue
and pelvic burns? What about the chipotle
chicken melt with guacamole ad right above
the "Merkins for Stars" article? And why
Evan Rachel Wood said no in *Mildred Pierce?*
And I'm thinking now about Rose,
what would she want?
Thinking about the word: *postiche,*
her thick lips, the tattooed X's
on her tough-woman fingers.

Lake is a red pigment

> Lake is a red pigment
> composed of a coloring agent combined, usually
> by precipitation, with metallic oxide or earth to
> create striking hues such as madder lake
> (a fierce yellow)
>
> —Patricia Hampl

I am a bastard.

I walk around in this body of mine.

After a year in the Asylum, I knew:

inside the body of my birthmother you find:

a letter folded/a globe/a life turned away from/

parts of my body/3 different names and towns.

I am earth and metal/the slag heap and the ore/

my blood fierce yellow—

the madder lake. Sometimes

I slide away. Sometimes I disappear.

I am truth, I am evidence.

Go West in memory of me.

My blood is the blood of work and making,

I can leave the body and become land.

I can make it all visible:

See it all: the red lake, how colorful I am.

She Set Me Swimming

Mary O'Shea cleaned houses for the rich—
she placed a fish in a body of water:
her child, my birthmother—she set me swimming.

My first house was a prison for children,
cast-offs and second-hands. I floated
on the surface of days, playing dead.

The spell of swimming can make an orphan dizzy—
moving through the spin/
to the plunge or the dip.

You don't know a thing until you're in it,
and maybe not even then. I found no home
in the house I was born in—

there was no real house on Cliff and Manilla—
just the hat-edge of the Hill, the brim of lonely.
I was locked up, and maybe

Mary O'Shea was locked up too—so,
woozy, bewildered, I lived for the trick:
the way to perform for the lifeguards of the body.

It would be 30 years before I knew my name, and
reeling, casting my line for love, I picked
nothingness as home.

I worked prisons, streets, and clinics—
trying to free children from the bodies
of men. Now I know something about what I did.

I'm still swimming for release,
to say the thing that springs me free.
If you want to do a good deed,

tend to the monsters inside you—
As for me, you don't know a thing about me,
walking around a stranger to yourself.

Dropping Blotter Acid at the Slag Dump

Out here on the perimeter there are no stars,
out here we is stoned, immaculate.

—Jim Morrison

In the field behind the shopping center,
at the slag dump on Rt. 51, down from Isaly's,
us working-class kids would hang.
We took our small bodies down
to watch the miraculous molten steel being dumped
from the railcars—there was nothing
like the exploding orange liquid against
the blue-black sky, nothing like the warm breeze
and smell of exhaust from passing cars. All our fathers were
steelworkers or factory workers and all we were
was bored-stoned, lying on our backs in the field
by the dump—but the night we dropped blotter,
it all jackknifed:
the steel sparked a firestorm of subatomic orange,
falling liquid stars over us, then oozing into new
rivers of running from my days,
from everyone—and then the breeze wasn't air,
but a floating man, a tree let loose from
its moorings, a glittering fire.
And at the same time, the wreckage of my days slipped
into the lovely,
just slipped right in into
quiet.
Is there a way you can know this?
I doubt it.
Does it matter?
No.
Then hours and hours and the jackknife back

into grinding gears, the machines, the dumping of fire
on that common Pittsburgh night.
Still.
I would like to be that still again, that one person
in a field of wild grass,
in the midst of nothing
but glittering.
In daylight, the slag cracked barren, volcanic, almost lunar—
mountain of slag, mountain of what we were made
of—Duquesne Works, Edgar Thompson,
Homestead Steel.
Rail cars operated by the Union Railroad
hauled molten slag to the growing mountain:
silicon, phosphorus, manganese, and limestone—
what was left from the open hearth.
By the time the dumping stopped in the 60's,
the mountain stood 200 feet high,
and covered the equivalent of 130 city blocks.
What did we know but steel and fire?
We'd wait for the jackknife—
watch those ladle cars slice up the sky, spill their load
down the mountain, cheering
for the red glow,
for the deaths we knew nothing about yet—
our fathers who would die of lung cancer,
emphysema from the mills—
the sweat and blood from all those bodies in the air—
taking in all that beauty,
washing it down.

2

When I get home from work
I'll call up all my friends
And we'll go bust up something beautiful we'll have to build again
—Jason Isbell

Praise Blue

Songs are like tattoos
You know I've been to sea before
— Joni Mitchell

I grew up in a double-wide of song and spirit,
she had me in a landslide
of happiness when

I grew my hair into hers—
long and straight so we could share a body.

I'm her jackknife, turning the blade back
onto prairies and wide open, so I can
make it true:

praise the body, praise blue,
my kidnapped story.

Just 20 when I decided
Joni Mitchell was my birthmother:
Underneath the skin/An empty space to fill in—

She's 8 years older than me—
I'm not stupid. I loved her traveling voice,
that's how we met, that's how I knew

she wanted me, and so she became
a child bride. Of course you're jealous,
I can't blame you, my body rocks the temple

of dignitaries and guitar slingers. I'm jacking
back—the blade towards you now. Everyone knows
it's not nice to point but

Jackson Browne was the one,
my 4 year-old father, I was his first song.

Praise the body blue.
Praise the jackknife of this lie,
my kidnapped story.

Surfing Cowboys

I walk into *Surfing Cowboys* on Venice Blvd
looking for abalone, the water stone that
balances matter and anti-matter—
& it can power a starship.
Oh.
I'm ready for the starship, to be a space-surfing
cowboy—
It's the grand water trine,
Jupiter, Saturn, Neptune aligned—
hasn't happened in more than a century.
My only other plan:
walk to "Morning Shot," the 40 ft. mural
on the corner of Speedway & 18th,
stand between Jim Morrison's big legs & wait
for instructions.
                    Have you ever felt flattened?
Even more—sunken in,
like you've been rode hard but not in a good way?
I've been looking for a change.
If the sea ears of the abalone can vibrate
with the chakras of my third eye, heart & solar plexus,
I'll wear it, I'll lick it daily like a lover &
shove it down my pants.
I love Cosmic Donna at *Surfing Cowboys* who says:
Where'ya from?
& when I ask her birthday,
it's the same day as mine.
Her iridescent eyes pull me in,
I say, *Same as Hendrix* &
she says, *Bruce Lee!* & I buy the ring.

I walk down to Maxwell's on Washington
for eggs & see the old woodframe paintings,
ships with sails billowing like sea balloons.
        Water everywhere:
metal stools covered with turquoise leather,
seats swimming green & the beat-up wooden counter.
I see the typewriter graveyard on the shelf by the register—
Life & death before me, the waitress in her skim hat,
ocean blue vest & cut-off shorts says,
Where'ya from?
Morrison is actually singing *People Are Strange*
on the music loop & in the next booth, a guy wearing
a tartan kilt & jet sunglasses, a tattoo sleeve
blue & black—some kind of mermaid with fish
flashing all around. I say, *I'm not from here.*
I bought this abalone at Surfing Cowboys
& I'm waiting for the starship.
She says, *Would'ya like some coffee?*
Sure, I say, waiting for my brother cowboys,
licking the abalone like a freak & staring at pictures
of the sea. I thought of the people I love
& what I hadn't done for them,
I thought of my body pulling me around.
I could see the rainbow doorway.
I could see the big waves coming.

The Snapping

Busted in Bakersfield, my '69 Chevy
with a dead transmission off I-40:
River Auto Parts & Marina.

    The guys in the garage said,
    You can crash here tonight—
    I called Michael, who flew in next day

with cash—1979, we hiked
into the brown hills outside of town,
dropped our gear in the dirt

to sleep under stars.   We were talking
about home, the long drive back, & I
thought of my father, who always said,

    Never have less than a half tank of gas.
    When you see the needle go below ¾—
    that's when you fill it.

I thought of visiting him
at Queen of Heaven Cemetery. I planted
the red geraniums he loved, my mother's

name on the joint headstone with the long ——
How could *she* be there with him,
her with her heartlessness?

It was not my place to say.

        I had no right—

She lived 15 years after him, then the dash
followed by the year 2000.

With all my blood & body, I wanted
them buried apart, I wanted
to spark him alive, feel his love & hear his sweet-

edged voice again.

> The skybowl full now with needles
> of light & the California air, moving free

Michael a ghost beside me,
nearly asleep when
the red line of eyes inched up the hill toward us.

He whipped off his belt, snapping &
snapping it to mimic gunshot,
to keep the roaming coyotes away.

We ran into the rocky dark, snapping & tripping,
but they wouldn't leave us be.
Tired, beatdown,

& all we wanted:
to sleep in peace in the California dirt ——
together, side by side.

The Boy from Hazard

I used to write stupid stories.
Like in one, I sold my Lamborghini
for $150,000—and then I shot this guy.
Really dumb stuff, but I just wanted
to write. I don't need much—
a car that works, a place to live,
some way to pay the bills.

I can't believe I'm crying
in front of you. I just feel bad
that you had a tough childhood and
my dad would come in every night and
push my hair out of my eyes—
because he cared and
I wish you had that.

But I heard stuff upstairs when I was young,
I think my dad wanted to be a cowboy
and he had his gun.
I would hear them screaming.
When he didn't get what he wanted.
He didn't hit her or anything but
I know she was really nervous,
took Xanax or something and now
the doctor said she can't just
get off of it.

Sometimes when she calls me
I can tell she's taking too many,
like she'll stutter or something or
talk funny. I hope you don't think I'm

saying you were a victim—
because I didn't mean that,
just that I don't want people
to treat each other badly.

Blue Rider

I met a descendant of Zebulon Pike in Santa Fe.
She told me she used to think a blow job
was when you went to the beauty salon to *get your
hair done, I mean your hair down there.*
She shared all this with her teenage friends,
& they believed. They had questions:
*If it's a dirty thing with boys, then why do you
go to the salon?*
She thought it was a blow/dye job, maybe
a *blue rider* [cobalt for the cold Colorado nights]
or a *low chaparral* [for the tough brush & desert
browns] One friend said: *I was always afraid
of it, but now I think I'll get a desert gold*
[landing strip the color of home-grown maize]
The burning question: if Pike's Peak is one of the
biggest cocks in the world
(highest of the southern Front Range)
then shouldn't there be a *fourteener?*
[thickest, tallest pussy hair west of the Mississippi=
bleached & snow-covered]
What would Zebulon say?
He was a fan of the front range, why not
the *pink granite* (sexier than potassium feldspar)
[pink front lawn with shaved steps to glory]
the chokecherry (for thorny S&M)
[dark red with a too-tight weave]
When she & her friends made appointments for blow jobs,
they sat under the dryers in the salon, their heads
fried. My friend, the descendant, found out about
sucking, became a blue rider, & the 14,115 ft. cock
of the Rockies erupted.

An eater, or swallowhole, is a reach of stream

An eater, or swallowhole, is a reach of stream
or a tidal area given to violent currents and waves that
often upset and/or suck under boats and kayaks and the
like as they are attempting passage.

—William Kittredge

The eater, my birthmother, was speaking:

> *I can't tell you his name.*
>
> *You have to promise me you won't look for him.*
>
> *He's not a nice man.*

Agitated, frenetic, the eater falling into her own waters.
Sobbing, almost wailing:

> *I'm so ashamed.*
>
> *I'm sorry.*
>
> *It was one night.*

I was swirling into the streambed,
lost in the downstream plunge.

I said:

> *Can you just tell me his name?*
>
> *I won't look for him.*

The eater filled with water, driving
toward the boulder's edge.

I rocked:

> into the lava break,
>
> into the fault.

Against Suicide

We tried to enter death and emerge from it—
we skin-popped it in our forearms, a few cents worth

　　　　—Luis J. Rodriguez

Because I used to start each day with thoughts of how
Because I used to sleep w/all my clothes
& shoes on
Because I love your hands,
your graceful fingers,
because fuck it—just wait
Because fuck it—just wait
Because your heart, exploding—
could open &
—yes, you have a right
—but the fire in you could talk
& blow up the dead
& lover, we've never
seen that yet—what
you will bring,
what firestorm of heart,
I'm waiting for it—
what patchwork of lives?

Taking Off, I Talk to the Dead

for Don

This place between rivers,
this runway now cradles me, and
I run down the list of those gone, but still
the ones who shelter me:

RT   Big Jim   Charlotte   Dorothy
—keep me safe.
The flight attendant says by mistake:
Enjoy your short life.

I mean, enjoy your short flight, she laughs.
Right the first time, I think—
then we are off to the quiet place,
the long familiar—sky   clouds.

In this place between rivers,
this runway time—
I miss you most, your sweet face,
your tender heart.

I think back to you at home,
sleeping on a single patch of king bed.
RT   Big Jim   Vee
Charlotte   Dorothy

I think back to this morning:
6:15 AM walking the jetway at
La Guardia—blue purple sky and
the blanket of calm:

enjoy your short life.
No one to say it to—
but here I am, sneaking around
in the night, city to city,

happy.

Wedding Shoes

Apart for the first time on our anniversary,
I was thinking of how we met: a dive bar
in Pittsburgh, you played lead guitar for the Hellhounds and
5 years later, Elvis married us in the Little White Chapel,
home of the 24 hour Drive-Up Wedding Window.
It was 106 degrees in Vegas.
In the lobby, he said:
I can't talk right now, my make-up's running.
I'll meet you in the chapel.
We bought the supreme package,
a video of the ceremony,
photos of Elvis next to his pink Cadillac, complete
with little white frames.
In the brochure:
We reserve the right to refuse service to anyone.
It was romantic.
The balding minister with the sides of his head dyed red
said: *Step up, step up.*
We've got another service in 10 minutes.
His assistant, a lovely woman in her 70's
dressed in gold sequins said,
God bless you, God bless you.
Elvis belted out *Fools Rush In* as we walked down
the gold-lamé-trimmed aisle:
I wore black and you wore two-tone wedding shoes—
black and white rockabilly suede.
20 years later, I was there, on another continent
feeling kind of sad and happy when you called, excited:
Hey, I'm playing a gig at the Handlebar—
it's a biker joint in Canonsburg—
I'm wearing my wedding shoes.

I Knew I Wasn't Poor

I knew I wasn't poor,
because I had a choice:
buy tampons or birth control pills.
I shoplifted.
When I opened the oven door,
splitting the closet-sized kitchen in half,
my only plan was heat.
The ice smooth on the inside of the windows,
the no money to pay the bill.
I knew I wasn't poor,
because I could always eat
at the restaurant where I waitressed.
I never went hungry.
I waited for the rich customer,
bored with her herb chicken—
to toss it: *No, I don't want to take it
with me. We're going to the theater.*
I secreted that half-plate of turned-
over food, and like a miser or explorer,
stashed it in my locker in the restaurant's
dark hallway. I had no shame, I was finding
my solution: how to eat, how to live,
I felt accomplishment. No insurance for
my beater car, I threw parking tickets in
the backseat with a flurry. I grew rich in
my imaginings. The People's Clinic when
I was too sick to last it out. I knew I wasn't poor,
and when my clothes wore raggedy and
I got angry at what I couldn't have, I walked
into the department store with an empty bag,
filling my heart, filling the holes
that were everywhere.

Muscle Beach, Venice, 2013

At Muscle Beach, the nautilus machines
empty on the rubber mats, one guy in a
bright orange speedo stumbles around,
in his 60's with a busted-up boom box
to his ear, he's weaving and half-dancing
to *Will You Be My Lucky Star?* On his arms,
big metal cuffs w/studs, veins sticking
out the front of his legs, a bunch of young
white guys come up with some dollars,
he snaps into muscleman pose and smile/
then back to weaving. Small poke in the front
of his sagging speedo, he's limping now,
breasts pancake-flat like an old woman's,
hair frizzed, big moustache. He bangs
the box when it cuts out, finds *Brick House*
and starts to snap dance, the Spanish girls
scream *Go, papi!* People are smiling, around
his neck a big gold Ganesha. Now he's walking
in circles between families and everyone staring.
He walks towards a woman and her stroller, wants
her to take a picture, give him money,
but she says, *no, no* and turns away, afraid.
5 feet later, I run into a rapper
with 4 layers of chains and beads
in 90 degree heat, black sunglasses with
heavy gold frames who says,
If you have bad moments, I can make them run
like water in the gutter.
No thanks, I say.
A tiny white dog rides by
in a bike basket, everyone cooing,

a hot man in a wet suit peeled down to
his navel, water dripping off his face,
carrying his surfboard. A woman in a
white uniform and purple suede boots,
a man in his 80's with a wide-brim straw hat
rolls the corner on an old-school bike, his cane
and clothes in the basket on back.
Signs that say: *Venice Beach Physicians* with
logo of hashish leaf underneath, *Just Get It!*
Young people outside dressed in neon green
hospital scrubs saying, *Come in.*
Skateboarder flies by, looks 20 but his face
so old, 50 ft palms line the ocean walk, seagulls
glide past, a Latino man on a segway and cell phone talking
loud, families and kids carrying orange beach towels,
lots of Spanish and someone skyriding over
the ocean with a yellow parachute.
The smell of dope everywhere.
I look back to see the orange speedo guy lying
on the weight pads, Morrison's voice deep
in the firmament:
This is the best part of the trip
This is the trip, the best part
I really like
What'd he say?

from *mad river*

If This Is Sex, It Must Be Tuesday

So it was every week on a Tuesday,
that you and your friend, Ginny,
strayed from the dance at St. Anselm's
to Duquesne Gardens, feigning interest
in hockey, waiting to get laid.
I can picture it—you in fake cashmere
with pearl buttons, a gabardine skirt
that hit you at midcalf, you and Ginny
shuffling popcorn till last period,
when you'd freshen your lips with TORRID RED
for the after game party at the Webster Hall dorms.
After all, these were the Pittsburgh Hornets,
this was 1951, and you were a poor Irish girl
from Garfield with a hard drive for excitement,
and hockey was it, getting cross-checked by the best,
having stories to tell in your lean, checkered life,
left with no father, a reluctant sister,
and a mother who cleaned houses for the rich.
So when did I happen, this one-night stand
with the MVP after his big, icy win,
the second Tuesday in February, or the third?
Do you remember the feel of his hands on you?
Were they rough, or tender, were they bloody
from fighting? And when your belly grew into
the body you never wanted, did you curse me,
try to cut me? Should I say you did your best,
a spare girl from a broken family,
or should I say it straight—
you wanted it, you took it, like we all do,
you lied to save yourself, you gave away
part of your heart, you couldn't
wish it right.

Mad River

Two dollars and sixty-five cents
at the Hot Spot Take-Out Shack
for one chili dog and a coke,
Birmingham, Alabama, 1979.
I kissed a Greyhound bus driver
too many times so I could eat,
I got one chili dog, I wanted two,
thought I'd get two. Lucky I'm not dead.
I asked him about his children, his
fourteen-year-old daughter saved my life,
pulled up his rotten conscience like
regurgitation, black bile memory—I said
How old is your daughter, afraid he'd want
more for his money, and in the slant light
of his dark Chevy he saw a slice
of my young girl face and said,
She's fourteen, I better get you back
to the depot, and the black stench
of his twisted conscience wanted one more
kiss, one more kiss to get me back
to the bus station and my long ride home,
to wanting to spit up the dark beans,
their reddish bodies staining my insides
like a dead baby, like a blood spill,
my heart pumping its mad river with
sixty cents in my pocket and twenty-six
hours till home, I prayed for rain,
I prayed for morning.

The Rolling Rock Man

It's not me shouting at no one
in Cadillac Square: it's God
roaring inside me, afraid
to be alone.
                    —Lawrence Joseph

Never talks, never tips,
drinks two Rolling Rock draughts,
maybe three as he sits for hours
in the restaurant, wears too many clothes
for the weather, his combat jacket,
his navy blue cap, oblivious
to the people eating lunch around him.
Can I get you something to drink? I say,
afraid to say, *How about a Rolling Rock,*
afraid to be familiar with a man like this.
Somebody already waited on me, he said.
Okay, good, I said.
You lost some weight.
Yeah, I said, *a little,*
amazed that he is speaking, that
he has noticed a change in me.
I look straight at him, one of his eyes
is blood, a red blotch from a punch—
he said, *You look like you have AIDS,*
you better go to the hospital,
you're gonna die soon.
I felt the evil wash over me
as I walked to my next table, stunned
by this backwash of words, this bold
sickness, this butcher world that's in
and around us, *Someone please, pray for us.*
Minutes later, he started shouting at no one,

Body bags, he yelled, *Body bags.*
I heard the words as I watched a five-year-old girl
stare at him, afraid for her. *Vietnam,* he shouted,
as women three feet away sucked Bloody Marys
and fingered their circle pins—he heard a song
and he spoke the words—I don't know
what he saw or heard.

Pittsburgh Poem

On Sarah Street, on the South Side,
the old woman stands with her broom, imagining
the air full of lug and swish from the steelworker's boot,
armies of gray lunchbuckets grace her thoughts
as she sweeps with the part of her that still believes;
sweeps while her sister makes paska and horseradish with red beets,
sweeps away the stains of a dead husband and a disappointing daughter.

She thinks of the dark well of J&L, how it sifted down to nothing,
the mill's hole of a mouth that ate full years of her life,
nights she pulled her husband from Yarsky's bar across the street,
him smiling like a bagful of dimes, half a paycheck spent,
the whole time, soot covering their clothes, the car, the windowsills
like disease, someone else's hands.

She holds tight onto the good times, the new green velour couch,
Saturday walks to the Markethouse for fresh red cabbage and greens,
trips to the Brown & Green store for new T-shirts, South Side windows
brimming taffeta and satin on the way to Mass at St. Michael's,
when the world was gleaming and available for one glorious day.

Now shadows angle across her print housedress and she holds tight
to her broom, hears her sister primping in the kitchen, smells the pea soup
with sauerkraut, the homemade mushroom gravy for perogies, she thinks
of the ten years since her husband died, of her daughter who calls
on holidays, she stands on her concrete lawn,
taking care of something invisible, the listless air,
her life.

Ravenous Blue

in memory of Scott Prather

We drive up to visit you, talking about school and work,
we don't say you've gone blind, we don't talk about AIDS.
In your mother's living room, you sit on a chair
with blue foam padding, your body too thin to bear
its own weight. I keep looking at the blue,
ravenous blue, remember? We were stoned and running
up and down the aisles of the beauty supply store,
looking for hair color, when I saw RAVENOUS BLUE,
and fell in love with the name.
You tried to talk me out of it, but we dyed
my hair from blond to blue, and shortly after,
young boys in leather started trying to pick me up,
mistaking me for a young thrasher.
The color was so dark, we couldn't cover it,
so we just laughed until it grew out, but
now we're here, just us and this pressing air,
your wide, blind stare, the words we don't say,
and I'm so sorry we are here,
and this is you,
dying.

Highway 99

Riding down Highway 99 on the back
of a cobalt blue Harley, no helmet,
with some guy named Wild Bill, my red
bandanna snapping in the hot night air,
a six pack of Pabst in the saddlebags,
I knew I had found the slick heart
of freedom, California style, on those
midnight roads from San Francisco to Fresno,
we were in-transit, strapped in by the wind,
and I wished my life on everyone breathing.

Just one hour into morning, my high fading
like a wicked joke, I slapped his back,
he yelled, *We're almost there.*
Five minutes into his faded pink trailer
on this cheap fifties mohair couch,
he pulls out a mugshot of himself, numbers and all.
Even through the beer haze, I knew I was stupid,
my wild self collapsing flat inside me, my heart
speeding into fear, as I said, *What were you
in for?* and he said, *Rape*, with a sick,
greasy smile like backwash, like a cold black
wave that made me look at the trees outside,
and I felt something hard rise inside me, like
another person, another me, and I asked him
if he'd ever want to hurt me—he hung his head
like a drowned man, said, *No, I guess not,*
and I said to his barrel chest, his huge arms,
that I wanted to go home, and then god picked up
my heart and we rode back, the sissy bar holding me,
and I couldn't think of one friend I had in life.

The bay looked like the only safe place,
dark and thick with the words of the ones
who never lived to say this—I'm telling you
so you'll know—that the black glue of the night,
the half-mast moon over a double line, the
cobalt blue couldn't bring me back.

Letter to Mario

Your hand goes up, your tone as earnest as an armed robbery.
I don't know your past, if you've killed or raped, you speak a
broken English, eyes alert as a found victim, this is maximum
security, this is you sitting in the back with your stack of books,
and me feeling my way through a dark hallway, and you are old,
with a steel wool mustache, spouting fractured words, jumble
of sounds, I strain to listen like a woman afraid
of intruders, ask you to repeat, and you do, again and
again and I look to the other inmates for help, and they shrug,
don't want to get involved, and say—*Nobody ever understands
him*—they have their own concerns, their short story
with a sick twist, their wounded poems, so I try to take
just one of your words and stretch it with a guess, expand
from the air, you shake your head and I know I haven't heard you
again—I can't cross this ground—I'm leaving you.
I am the next, the one more, another who hasn't heard you,
I move on because the rest of the class is bored, and
I don't know what else to try, and what else is there
to say—that your trust was sniped and gutted as a child,
that the prison wants you to rot, that I'm drowning in my own
thick limits, and all I can feel are your earnest eyes, and
this is not good enough, not even close, and here it is again,
us and them, and I can see why you'd hate, in this brick, cold
house in another country, and no syllables we say, no longing
for gods and revolutions can set it right.

An Abortion Attempt by my Mother

Rolling side to side in my warm mother,
the juices of life pulsing through my veined skin,
wild juices of calves' tongues and loose
stretchy kid skin like young gray wrens.
I drink unborn water in the Garfield back room
in the dark while my mother cries.

The prodding of wolves' teeth,
eyes red and ailing, the shaking
of orange clay and cracked slate, the loosening,
exposing the underground creatures to full sky,
the greased worms are screaming, the dead moles stay dead.
This is the feeling.

Sucking

Sap is running out of the pine trees
like cum—and I know someone is coming right now,
screaming pleasure while I walk on this gravel path,
while insects stick in this golden sap of tree wound,
someone is sucking on someone's breast, someone's cock, lost
in the original comfort, lips urging and repeating
like every blue vein, while grey bark falls dead from trees
and everything fills with blood, the renegade stream
that cuts through the length of night
as we walk around alone
we suck the air
we suck on nothing.

Saving the Crippled Boy

Tenth-grade field trip, I'm stuck
in the back of the chartered bus
with one-armed Bob Saunders, ten
rows away from the waves of my friends.
There I was, sharing the seat
with his hook of a hand,
his flesh-colored arm-like arm,
was it plastic, what was it made of,
we were sixteen, but it wasn't just
his arm—he was short, his hair
was greasy, he wouldn't talk to anyone.
And who would ever love him, had he ever
kissed a girl—would he ever kiss anyone?
Years before I knew about *mercy fucks*,
somewhere between New York City and Hampton,
it started, and we necked all the way home
from Springdale, the whole time, the bolts
in his arm clicked on the rim of the bus window,
Bob's tongue poking and pushing like
a hyperactive worm in my mouth, me afraid
his arm would flap over me like a hard dead person,
the whole time my good deed burying me, I wanted
to save him, just to save him, and now we were
both alone, covered with our benchwarmers,
Bob half on top of me in the cold vinyl seat,
I felt him get hard—small and hard, and
what had this become, I wanted blazing sanctimony,
saving the crippled boy with each plunge of
my normal tongue, but now I was saying, *Look,*
this is what you can't have, not for real,

this *is* for *today*, and I grew small and hard,
and thought of my boyfriend at home, my best
friend, Patty, and my sick, ailing heart.

after sex on a train

canadian rockies fill
my window I am naked
eating blueberry muffins
sipping coke and smelling sperm
lakes and pines no birds fly past
I think of wild blueberries
bleeding juice through pale yellow
the yellow that's almost white
my calves bruised from holding on
rivers moving swollen white
rail ties lie in piles and I
sniff the musk that we all want
telephone poles bending toward
water the white birch the pines

A Waitress' Instructions on Tipping or Get the Cash Up and Don't Waste My Time

Twenty percent minimum as long as the waitress doesn't inflict bodily harm.

If you're two people at a four top, tip extra.

If you sit a long time, pay rent.

Double tips for special orders.

Always tip extra when using coupons.

Better yet, don't use coupons.

Never leave change instead of bills, no pennies.

Never hide a tip for fun.

Overtip, then tip some more.

Remember, I am somebody's mother or daughter.

No separate piles of change for large parties.

If people in your party don't show up, tip for them.

Don't wait around for gratitude.

Take a risk. Don't adjust your tip so your credit card total is even.

Don't ever, ever pull out a tipping guide in public.

If you leave 10% or less, eat at home.

If I call a taxi for you, tip me.

If I hang up your coat for you, tip me.

If I get cigarettes for you, tip me.

Better yet, do it yourself.

Don't fold a bill and hand it to me like you're a big shot.

Don't say, *There's a big tip in it for you if* . . .

Don't say, *I want to make sure you get this*, like a busboy would steal it.

Don't say, *Here, honey, this is for you*—ever.

If you buy a $50 bottle of wine, pull out a ten.

If I serve you one cocktail, don't hand me 35 cents.

If you're just having coffee, leave a five.

from **boneshaker**

Machine Shop of Love

I like the way you play your guitar.
That's what I said the first time we met—
there's no explanation for being this corny—
just love or deception.
So,

             under the viaduct,
        under the old/railroad bridge of our ancestors/
        immigrant steelworkers/slaves of Carnegie/
        we rocked the back seat of a '69 Chevy/
        you pulled my chuck taylors/your jeans were long gone/
        goodbye to cotton/the rolling stones teeshirt/
        we're spinning in lust and oh
        steamy back windows and nothing
        can stop it/the rolling and tearing/
        machine shop of love, love—

its big plans/blue eyes/its you/
looking straight through the body/
in search of the heart/for two
weeks I waited until I proposed/
Let me think, you said/but no—

                the body,
it has its own light/own scent/
own can't-turn-your-back-on-it-glue/
I'll wait, I said, and did—

            for the touch

of your hair, the tender of hands/I love
the way you play your guitar/
compression/precision/the rock &
burn of it/the playing the/*yes*, you said—

Penitentiary

My name is Gale, you whisper.
I step back, you step forward.
I'm inches from your pasty skin, your
ice-blue eyes. *Where are you from?*
Philadelphia, I lie, in case you
remember, in case you ever get out.
You know I'm lying. You know my working-
class shoes, my cheap Lerner's dress,
my predictable blonde hair. You're 65/
I'm 23 in the old men's colony.

Warden says:
Don't worry, Gale never
speaks above a whisper to anyone.

I get to know you in the scan & rattle
of facts in your file:

> *4 years old beaten & molested/*
> *State Children's Home till 16/*
> *convicted at 18/sodomy of minor/*
> *victims 3-8 years/convicted/murder*
> *first degree/neighbor boy raped &*
> *strangled in bushes behind home*

The boy/in the bushes/his tiny body/
what/did you whisper/when you strapped/
his neck down?

The next time I see you/day after lockdown/
one of my clients/one of your friends/

raped & strangled/tangled in bedsheets/
belt cinched around his neck/in his cell/
Who do you think did it?
you ask as you walk up behind me.

I turn to see your eyes, everything
I'm afraid of: the salesman in the 5&10,
his misshapen head, eyes darting
like stray bullets; the old man downtown
who followed my Catholic girl uniform,
shoved his knee between my legs;
the man who put the ladder to my window &
masturbated on the brick/sperm on the mortar/
sperm on the mortar/

I don't want to help you/I don't want to
look/
                    knowing you were murdered/
                    as a small child/poor small boy with no heart/

        I'm looking for the name/of the first/
        person who hurt a child/

I was born with chances/were you born with none—
still I close my heart:

When I tell the warden
I don't want to help you/when I pull
my hair back/when I keep my eyes
down/when I quit my job/
when I see you again

& again in my dreams, a ghost
plays a white fiddle: all our sins
over & over in a thin whine.

My Mother and Aunt Charlotte Talk Disasters at Schmotzer's Village Bakery

Did you read that when they found him,
he was missing both arms? My mother eyes the nut horns.

Isn't that awful, and he had a ten-year-old daughter
who identified the body, can you imagine?

My mother squeezes the sandwich buns, frowns.
I'll tell ya, if you don't get here before 10:00

on senior citizen's day, there's nothing left.
I know, said my Aunt, *Did you hear they found*

the black box for flight 800? She turns to the cashier
and says, *Are you all out of sliced egg bread?*

My mother heaves a sigh toward the sweet rolls:
Those kids saved for two years for that trip

with bingos, car washes. You never know when
you're gonna go. She orders some sticky buns.

Aunt Charlotte settles on the sliced white:
Mildred, they found his arms in a trash bag,

stuffed in a dumpster, can you imagine?
I knew they'd find them. A pair of arms.

You go outside to empty your trash and see arms.
I can't believe this, will you look at these

shelves? Now there's nothing left for us.

Going Deep for Jesus

> Run to the street light, make a right
> at the blue car, and go deep
>
> —Sharan Watson

1981, I'm on the back of a cherry
red Kawasaki with my boyfriend Stush,
my biker jacket bought with a tax return
from a year of waiting tables, stuffed
in my pocket the bad check I wrote
to see Stevie Ray play the Decade.
Down Beck's Run we hit Carson, my cheek
resting on Stush's firm shoulder till
the ground rises up with the hulk of J&L
across the river, steel house that burns it all,
an up-against-the-wall-fuck, thick &
ripping, everything is smokestacks
& yellow blaze. We ride the river roads,
looking for deserted two-lanes,
newspapers stuffed under our leather
for warmth. I want to forget my name—
everything but the sharp lean into
the next turn, the cheap slap of the wind.
Stush brags about his water-cooled,
two-stroke engine, but I just want
the contact high of leather, metal,
and the slow burn of a few joints.
Past the bridges & bridges, we ride
away from our fast-food jobs and
run-down apartment, toward the smell
of the Ohio, its perpetual mire, the rotting
docks and lean-to's, *to what we knew.*
I knew the muscles in his back & his

low voice would make me come
back to my self. We stop near the bog
of the river's edge to have hard sex
on the ground, our jeans still on,
trying to shotgun a moment, to split open
our lives in the brilliant light until
we *were* the mills, we *were* the fire.
It was then I decided god and orgasm
were the same thing, that if jesus
had an address, it would be a dark two-lane,
if god were here, she'd shove down
like a two-stroke in a rainstorm,
she'd let it fly.

Poetry Workshop at the Homeless Shelter

So I'm the white teacher reading
some Etheridge Knight poems to the four
residents who showed: *For Black Poets*
Who Think of Suicide—thinking
these guys have seen it all and want
something hard-core, when a black man
named Tyrone raises his hand:
These poems offend me.
They do? I say. Yes, I was raised
not to curse, and I don't see why
a poem has to use those words.

What poems do you like?
Langston Hughes.
Yeah, someone else says, Jean Toomer, man.
Tyrone says, *Let's talk about calculating a poem.*
Pardon me, I say—
You know, cipherin a poem—
Why don't you show me?
Tyrone draws this two dimensional
image of this three dimensional grid, based
on numerology, he says, in which each letter
of the alphabet corresponds to a number.

Look, it's like you start
with a 13,25, then go to 8,5,1,18,20—
that's the start of my first line:
'My heart opens to the new world'—See?
I am stunned by it all—strange genius
or just strange? How long
have you been writing this way?

All my life, but nobody understands it,
I got boxes in my room filled with calculations,
I got plays and soap operas, and one day
I'll sell them.

I'm looking into Tyrone's eyes, beautiful
savant, wondering what to say:
I'm standing here in my new Levis and
Chuck Taylors, knowing I don't understand
either, and his desire humbles me.
Class is ending so I ask him to bring
more next week, but he has to see
his caseworker about his bad leg,
jammed up in a streetbeating in Philly.

Now I'm walking out of the shelter,
my white skin reminding me how wrong
I am most days, thinking about his sweet
numbers, his poems luminous with industry.
I'm opening the door to my car, counting
vowels: 13,25,8,5,1,18,20, my heart
stirring in the new world.

My Father Teaches Me Desire

Once it starts you can't stop it:
My father leans into it like a hunchback
at the particle-board table in the light
of our kitchen, arranging his little world:
Vidalia with paring knife; Iron City next
to French's; open sardine tin/no plate.

His left hand grabs the onion/the right
slashes a fat slice/the right dips into
the briny swamp of sardine/lifts one
by the tail/down to the French's/then
plunges it headfirst into his cavernous mouth.

Crunch of Vidalia, then pump an Iron, and
we are livin now, baby, we are home—
me watching my Dad from the dining room,
the grunt and slosh of it all, thinking,
My god, he's eating the head—where
are its eyes?

What world is this? He's god and brute,
half quake/half precision, what kind of man
can stare down the milky eye of the sardine
sans flinch, then sever its head with
those same incisors he grew in his mother's belly?

Now he's starting again, reaching
for the onion, two-fisted and ravenous,
king of kings in this 6x6 tabernacle,

he's the holy spirit of torque and focus,
and this is more action than
I've ever seen in church.

I'm standing here at age 12, learning
that sweet seduction of revulsion/desire,
I'm learning real good that the guy I want
to marry is the one who can do the worst
thing without blinking, a man who eats life
raw, the heads of things—and what else
won't scare him?

Oh Father, oh terrible primate, I am one of you.
Together we can skin the rabbit, stuff
the apple in the pig's mouth, in this kitchen
there is so much I don't know yet:
That I can write this poem.
That I will want to die many times in this life.
That in ten years I will drive back to this house,
to this kitchen, looking for your glasses.
I'll drive back to you at the funeral home
and gently place them on your face
in the casket, with no flash
or fanfare, just the music
of my heart playing:
too soon,
too soon.

Near the Foundling Home

1.

Mother of Blood, Mother of Skin, I don't know
whose life I'm in: *Adopted's not chosen but plucked
from some womb/and still I'm the wren
on the porch looking in.*

2.

Did anyone's heart have to break just to make me?
And which is the place that holds me to the ground?
I'm writing these lines, I'm shooting for the wild
heart of accident and still you have no face/
mother/it's 4:00 AM I'm rabid with my own
heart/empty & full with the shape of your face/
I'm starving, mother, in my no/story, speaking
to the no/one of you.

3.

Do you know the yellow scarf of grief, how it hangs
or saves you? It could come tonight/ten years
from now on any street: I walk in the still/born
night and there you are: air packed tight with
bone/hair/your hands first touching me/
I twirl to the huge zero of you, into all
your faces lining my dreams like barnacles/
now we're beyond the lump in the throat
to the shaking at night till my lover stops me—
nothing wrong—my bones shaking yesterday/
back to today, this time worse,
this time you:

4.

Mother of Blood feeding the tremor,
mother of rupture, bruise & shudder;
Phantom; Specter; Apparition;
Fracture & hoard; Quake & splinter.

5.

Just fill the "never" of looking like
anyone. Give me the story, broken & beautiful:
give me the body parts, detailed & sweet,
till there is nothing, nothing left faceless.

                Tonight I would say:
Tell me what the air felt like the last day
you held me, the snatch of lilacs that
brushed the dormer at the foundling home,
how its sweetness hung thick in the air
like a ticket out, all the hands, the boys'
hands you'd lose yourself in those nights
you'd sneak out, the magnolia talc and
rosewater you'd smooth on your skin,
trying to make one summer night
last a year. How much you lost.
When our skin finally touched,
didn't you know you were home?
Tell me: What happens to the body
when you hand your child over—
does it shake—or recoil into snake?

6.

Mother of Blood, purging its young;
Mother of Skin, Guardian of Scars:
See Flush for atonement; see Purify
for evacuation, see Exile, Expel, see
free and clear.

7.

Tonight I'll tell you the lie of the story:

> It was sky blue.
> A sitting room with one rocking chair
> and your hands, large and soft, cupping
> my head of no hair. And every time you
> whispered, your voice covered me
> like a warm stream and no one else was
> alive or dead. And when you whispered
> goodbye, it sounded like every other word
> and that warmth never happened again.
> Then there was nothing, then nothing, and
> nothing for a very long time.

My Father Teaches Me to Dream

You want to know what work is?
I'll tell you what work is:
Work is work.
You get up. You get on the bus.
You don't look from side to side.
You keep your eyes straight ahead.
That way, nobody bothers you—see?
You get off the bus. You work all day.
You get back on the bus at night. Same thing.
You go to sleep. You get up.
You do the same thing again.
Nothing more. Nothing less.
There's no handouts in this life.
All this other stuff you're looking for—
it ain't there.
Work is work.

Boneshaker

Sometimes you just have to cut & run.

         *   *   *

I was in the virgin court, sweet flower
at the feet of the May Queen—and
beating up boys in the playground, I was
a pitiful 35 on the shrink's GAF scale
(global assessment of functioning):
defiant at home/poor impulse control/
my wild girl fire was spinning—
they told me to shut up, be sweet, keep
your shirt on—I laced my black hi-tops,
loaded my cousin's shotgun.

         *   *   *

Don't lose your place.

   Stand in line to see
   the priest each day. He hugs us
   too tight, too long.

   Mrs. Reid ties us to chairs,
   hits us with rulers
   for flirting with boys.

   The diocese says: *these*
   are the movies good catholic girls should see.

Say your prayers.

I learned the prayer of men hurting girls:

> say hi to the nice man/be polite/
> forget the torn jeans open-road
> open-mouth-insert-cunt—any girl
> who says cunt
> is one.

When my old man neighbor
tried to kiss me,
I remembered my place, 15 years old,
it was second.

*   *   *

Did I say there's no place for a girl to live in this country of fear?

*   *   *

In the small place,
the fetus of the world's inside you growing:
clot of its bloody voice;
it's the size of a seed,—turning
your body against itself, cave
of uterus filling with blood of
world, world, baby fetus,
there, there.

You can never go back to your young girl fire, apple tree, fat
spring air.

*   *   *

Girl in the wardrobe mirror.
Stares into the eyes of no one she knows.

Did you think you couldn't crumble?

You decide your breasts are repulsive.
There is no one as ugly as you.
You decide to break yourself.

Girl in the wardrobe mirror,
slams her arm against the door, forearm
hits the dark wood, Again, Again,
swinging the door on its hinge until
the body answers: *exquisite*,
until the yellow-green bruise and she is
home again in her body.

Blue girl, this is your new bruise.
This is your torn-jeans-open-road.
This will give you something no one
can take, something of your own
to watch over. Something to mother.

* * *

You keep cheap wine in your closet,
and valium for when your boyfriend comes.

He broke up with *you*, but every week
he picks you up & fucks you
in his car—in the backroad parking lot.
You pretend he loves you.

* * *

You turn towards him
in the backseat of his beat-up buick:
you see his mouth yawing & yawing &

no sound

the fat palm of his hand's
coming at you/shoving
your head down/open your mouth
his cock jams your mouth full/

again/again/you're back in the mirror/
you slam his cock to the back of your throat/
you don't care where your mouth is,

                    *   *   *

Now you got it, girl, you're starting to leave the body/
bathe in its sensation/drug it
so the pain stays dull/
where do you go?

In the space between
the hand clutching the car door & the floating off,
it's hard, isn't it, because it hurts too much, there was a man once
who scared you, there was a man a thousand times who scared you, ask
any woman,

She'll say: *He turned into someone else, he wouldn't stop, he grabbed me.*

                    *   *   *

When you leave the body, where do you go?

To a blue bruise/second grade/click of new shoes?
Apples/chiffon/the dead?

no

       you've got to

say that sliding

          goodbye to the body and go

        * * *

Bitch, don't go crazy on me.

But you don't hear him, because the body,
your body in the backseat
is starting to break away,

and you see the body translucent(your body)
on the vinyl, legs splayed open and the body(your body)
full of water, so full you are a fish holding
an ocean inside,

        you see your skin breaking apart, and there's
water everywhere, and blood, and the world's
in a sac on the floor,

        you watch yourself pick it up, watch
as you bring it to your teeth, bite the sac open,
a thousand voices spill out onto the floor.

* * *

Floating

    now

    above your body, you see

so much water, washing the body,

      washing the dead world,

         you are

    water

      open mouth

sky

My Father Teaches Me Light

7 AM I get the call you have died.
To get to the hospital before my mother &
sister & their arsenal of sorrows:
I rush to your bedside, nothing
has ever been this important.
I'm standing in the shaft of morning,
the light through the window splitting
the room in half: the dead body of you/
the living me. I talk to the air, tell you
it will be alright, look to the ceiling
for floating bodies: there is no you there.
The part of me in your heart, where is it?
And what is the body now, old empty house?
You said you'd come to haunt me,
pound your cane on the floorboards,
I'd hear you say, *Pay your bills!*
I hang your cane on my bedroom door,
I wear your VFW jacket & sometimes
old men stop me to make sure I'm not
mocking the War. I want to tell them:
You were the one who spun me into the fire
of myself; I am the one you left behind,
the one you saved while you were here.

Zen of Tipping

My friend Lou
used to walk up to strangers
and tip them—no, really—
he'd cruise the South Side,
pick out the businessman on his way
to lunch, the slacker hanging
by the Beehive, the young girl
walking her dog, and he'd go up,
pull out a dollar and say,
Here's a tip for you.
I think you're doing a really
good job today. Then Lou would
walk away as the tippee stood
in mystified silence. Sometimes
he would cut it short with,
Keep up the fine work.
People thought Lou was weird,
but he wasn't. He didn't have much,
worked as a waiter. I don't know
why he did it. But I know it wasn't
about the magnanimous gesture,
an easy way to feel important,
it wasn't interrupting the impenetrable
edge of the individual—you'd
have to ask Lou—maybe it was
about being awake, hand-to-hand
sweetness, a chain of kindnesses,
or fun—the tenderness
we forget in each other.

Cruising the Blue Belt

Driving 51 North to Pittsburgh,
I saw the graffiti chalked on the underpass:

Things to do:
1. Kill Satan
2. Free Larouche
3. Buy milk

At last! I thought,
someone who thinks like me!
No, it's not that I want
to kill Satan or free Larouche,
it's that list—the things
we want to do each day,
how do you make it?

When you stop and realize
that even Satan-killers
need to think about milk,
it really takes you back.

And what *should* my list be
on an average day in this aching world:

1. Kill Rush Limbaugh
2. Find a cure for AIDS
3. Buy chocolate

Sounds just as stupid as the Larouche thing
—that's my point—
Like when I was driving home

after teaching a class on meter
in poetry, and feeling pretty good
about it, too—Terry Gross
had to come on *Fresh Air* and talk
about gangs in L.A.—and my list
for the day, which had been:

1. Prepare for class
2. Go work out
3. Meet Carole at Ali Baba's

—my list became silly, shallow—
and why was I on the planet anyway
and what was my *real* list?

Like the time I met my husband
for lunch downtown, and, you know,
we were in the mood for Italian, something
with fresh basil and garlic, as we walked
past the YMCA on the way to Oxford Center,
there was a woman and her child wrapped
in dirty pink blankets, lying smack
against the wall with mounds of brown
paper bags around them, and what was I
thinking about—

Your list? None of
my business—but I'm asking.
Have you found a way
to walk around the world, have you
found a way to negotiate the pain? And

where do you hold it, the pain, and please,
if you find that list, scratch it
on the underpass next to Satan, and
leave your name, please,
leave your name.

from *red sugar*

I Saw One of Blake's Angels

at the peep show on 10th/singing her
angel song/she was passing through
the ring between heaven & hell/flames
at her feet & men with long fingernails
& grabbing mouths. Beautiful.
She was

transparent with a fire beneath her skin,
her thighs titanic, she was innocence &
experience her mouth the only o in prophesy,
she would fly around the room with her eyes.
My name is Angela, she said, *I can talk when
I'm doing things, what do you want?*
She is

lying back on the pink mohair
pillow/legs spread wide to pink/exposing
the history of Occidental morality with
a small shaved V of wild red/left breast
longer than her right/hanging down like a
nozzle, like rubber/that crazy orangey-
brown/she is

ecstatic in her own longing/18
max/slippery floor/guy down the dark hall
jerking off on the wall/in the fluid stages of
empire & slavery/I like to look at her. I speak
to the phone by the cum-smeared plexiglass/
she is

nearly mythical in her longings, her
boyfriend, new job: *We're getting married
in June/Great*, I say, : *I can play with myself
if you want/Okay*, I say, just like the guardians of
tradition/she passes the glittery pink scarf over
the wild V/pinching her nipples like only
an angel can & giggling: *like this?*
she is

        lifting both feet to the plexiglass/one
inch from my face is her angel-of-blake pussy/
licks her middle finger & shoves it in/working
the only water pump in heaven/screen's sliding/
I'm bending/more quarters
                  & slides &

she is

        singing in a voice to revive
        all the dead:
        is this it?,
                sweet song:
                        is this what you want?

she is

        tracing the pink/of her thighs
        with small pink hands:
        do you like that/
                like that?
                she is the next circle of hell/
                the one where

                         I know
we either stay or go today/no other day/
my face pink in the dark/her dark pink
track lines/we meet in her body/
                                    together
we roll the dark angel of death/take her
pocket change & prop her

                    /wedged/
in the dirty corner/we pass the row of lockers/
walk the hallway of swords/the line of hollow-
eyed men/the old woman gatekeeper, wooden
with a face painted gray/
                         we, incandescent
                  & bereft/can see the door open/curb

                  of the outside world, our bodies
spinning into the searing white of the afternoon/
after a good night of drugs/we are triumphant
in the downtown litter/
                         I am stunned to find
my own loneliness & magnificence, here/
with her/in my body.

Lip

Edge, verge, labium. Flange, impertinence, recompense.
Road to the mouth inside us, the blue-red slippery,
the not quite in. Insolence, convexity, lip lip
rim. Body collar, curb of the pussy, furbelow, flounce.
Skirt of the known world, threshold to the threshold,
trim. Margin of the valley between thighs, sidle up/
jump. Brink of your first happiness, almost
oops, you're in/edge on.

liplipliplip/bopbopaloobop/as good as dope/almost.
The swoop, the junction, the original front lawn,
one less than a trois, spank it, frisk it, the light goes
on. Sidewise smile, gateway to red. Light summer
jacket & your mama said: save it for a rainy day,
wear a light jacket on a summer night, but she
never rocked the body electric, original e, she
never sang it like that/did your mama? Ever
turn over, drive right up to the window,
say, I'll take some. Give me some spurt, some
rush, some one more time, some honey,
I'm the city, I don't need your map.

Shooter

I shoot the old man who followed my 11-yr-old body on Smithfield St/because
I smiled at him/because it was Xmas/I shoot the man who jacked-off/on
the bricks of our house/put a ladder to my window when I was 12/I shoot the
professor who said my work was illogical, then used me for publicity when I
won an award/the businessman who wanted to talk about my teenage
breasts/I'm loading & re-loading/the guy who walked up to me when I was
a cashier & asked about my "hole"/I hope you still like me when I say the
gynecologist stuck his tongue down my throat when I was 16/the writer who
read his gang rape poem to a room of women students/I'm putting my finger
on the problem/the men who pose as feminists/the predators/the rapists/the
bullies & thugs among us/my uncle who tried to kiss me when he was
drunk/my 60-yr-old neighbor who grabbed me when my parents weren't
home/it was my fault/a man named Roy who wouldn't stop when I said no/he
said *shut up*, he said *now*/he taught me to love the trigger/I'm shooting the
cook who grabbed me from behind in the restaurant kitchen/the famous poet
who said there are no great women writers/the boyfriend who left his handprint
in black & blue/the men who say we're too serious, prettier when we smile/I'm
smiling & shooting/the shrink who tried to lock me up/the boss who gave me a
ride home/wanted a blow job/pushed my head down/the poet who said I didn't
praise him enough/here's one for you/the restaurant manager who told me
to grow a thicker skin & wear a skimpy uniform/because really we have an
attitude/we need to lighten up/I shoot all the men I've left off the list, so I don't
have to worry my pretty little head about it.

Red Sugar

You walk inside yourself on roads and ropes of blood vessels and tendons,
you walk inside yourself and eat weather

        —Gretel Erlich

When I was young, I was a comet
with an unending shimmering tail,
and I flew over the brokenness below
that was my life. I didn't know until I was
twelve that we carry other bodies inside us.
Not babies, but bodies of blood
that speak to us in plutonic languages
of pith and serum. When I was
six, there was a man in the woods,
naked. I didn't know him, but I knew
he was a wrong kind of man/so I ran.
With my inside body I see his skinny
white bones and curled mouth, he looks
like sickness and it's the body inside me
that's running, my red sugar body
that shows me the brutal road to love,
the one good man, the one song
I can keep as mine. I heard it once
when I was waitressing, something
made me turn my head, made me
swivel to look at a woman across
the room, wasn't even my station,
but the red sugar said, *go.* When I
saw her up close, I knew she was
blood. I can't explain this—I only met
my mother once. I said, *Do you know*
a woman named Dorothy? Her face
was pale, she said, *No*—in that hard way.
Maybe her red sugar told her to run—

but before she left, she grabbed my arm,
said, *I did have a sister named Dorothy,*
but she died. Two inches away from her
dyed blond hair, I said, *okay,* but both
our inside bodies knew she was lying.
Some people call it *eating weather*—
the way you swallow what you know,
but keep it—later it rises like a storm
from another world, reptilian and hungry.
It's the thickness that drives us and
stains us, the not asking/just coming/
the cunt alive and jewel-like/the uncut
garnet and the lava flow/it's barbarism/
bloodletting/the most liquid part of us/
spilling/spreading/the granular red sea
of sap and gore/sinking/moving forward
at the same time/slippery/red
containing blue/it's the sweet,
deep inside of the body.

The Phenomenology of Sex

I tell my friend Jude
about the phenomenologist I'm dating:

> We were doing poppers in Texas
> in his living room & on our knees
> having sex—I turned around to look
> just before the big O & saw him
> chewing the wooden arm
> of the easy chair.

And then you broke up with him?

  No. I didn't get the message.

I tell her how he talks phenomenology to me:
how consciousness is everything, how important it is
to suspend assertions of existence independent of consciousness,
which I take to mean, he's afraid of living.

Jude says:
> the bottom line is he's chewing
> on the chair. What are you gonna do?

I tell her how, in Pittsburgh, he tried
to teach me how to drive my own car.
How I said to him: if this car crashed in a forest,
    you couldn't hear it, but I would.

So that was it?

  Yeah, that was it.

When Foucault Entered the Body

My friend Aaron said he'd like to give Sean Penn
a tongue bath, & I guess that's clear enough,

but I want more. I want to wear men's shoes
because they're stylish, sturdy—& just because

I think Patricia Arquette's beautiful
doesn't mean I want to be her. Just give me a wife

beater & an AK-47 & I'll be Nic Cage
bustin up Con-Air, fuckin A. You can call me

shallow, but in grad school the main theoryhead
called me late at night for advice about his boyfriend

& that's when Foucault entered the body—
give me a break with his "I'm not speaking" routine.

Nobody wants to inhabit his/her own body
all the time—Take my friend Aaron, for example.

When he's irritated, he says, "panties, panties, panties"
& that helps calm him down. & just because

my husband had to explain Popa Chubby, the Blues singer,
to me—doesn't mean I'm naïve—just on vacation.

Why stay in the body & miss the ricochet back in,
the cool body return with its jolt of red sugar

& don't you just love the inside out of it?
The veins & pink slippery animal openings of it?

Panties, panties, panties.

When I dress in drag, honey, I'll be in a pink-flower-

prom-gown with a motherfuckin tiara—

because a sharkskin suit would be too much

like home.

The Day I Stripped

down to nothing, his tongue wormy in my throat—it was my first
visit & my gynecologist grabbed my sweetness, said,
Don't tell anyone. His apey arms still covering me, I popped
back outside to my friend Craig in his blue Impala (I didn't have a car) &
I remember what I was wearing, the green & white checkered
girlie shirt (bright, lively) & he said, *How'd it go?*

Fine, I said, & we headed home. 51 south around Maytide &
I had to pee, so we stopped at Joey Carbone's Cocktail Lounge
(really a low-level strip joint) & when I wandered the brown hallways
in my suburban belted coat, one of the girls popped
her head out of a doorway like a bad-ass gidget & said dirty loud:
You the new dancer?

& for a second I was that wild & flexible &
could she see the stripper in me? The doctor's squirmy tongue was still
licking. I wanted to be what she needed & now I was qualified. Something
had happened to her I bet, no one
gets to look so hard so young unless—I said No,
I'm looking for the bathroom.
> > > *Jesus Christ!*
> > > she said, *Where the hell is she?* & popped
> > > back to her cave.

Years later when they closed & the strippers went down the street
to Stiffy's & their johns or back to being stay-at-home moms, the
workers were stripping the paint from the joint's marquee—& quit one day after half
the name & for 24 magnificent hours, the building existed as "Joey Carbone's Cock"
& not cocktail lounge & it was withered, flaky, but big—
for the first time, as big as he said it was.

Red Song

There's a great river running under me
a red song for the babies
bloody turnips on the infant tree
I'm tired of the ruin
and the artichokes with their fibrous heads
and I could say distantly: *the aisles of the world
are glutted with blood and rutabagas,*
and *see the entrails of birds hanging
from the clotheslines of the rich and despondent,*
and that would sound like Neruda
but not nearly as good, and I'm not caring—
just this: they were moving in me
        there were three

Serum

It is another of the old alchemical truths that
'no solution should be made except in its own blood.'
    —Nor Hall

I was afraid I had changed. I felt like table salt instead of the red tomato,
the thin reed at the side of the water & not the water. In night dreams
no longer was I chasing the bad man through the dark woods &
stabbing him—now I was in a world of wood & glass—
the insides of the world were missing—I was a passenger
riding up & down grey streets & there were no fires.
I wanted to be the red sugar of the pomegranate—open me up & all
my beautiful seeds there for you.

    I encountered the dead & they seemed to have more power in an
    offhand turn of the head than I did in my distant stare.

        You could say I was meeting my own death in the dream, blah, blah.
        I'm telling you my dreams used to be liquid, morphy & cinematic—you
        could feel the blood (red sugar) when you were shot—it was swampy, savage,
        real & surreal, fleshy & red.—it was hemorrhage & blight, but in a good way.

                    x   x   x

In the hospital they lifted my uterus like a suitcase
of knobs & tubers, threw it in a haz/mat bin.

    Forget what you know about orderly living rooms,
there were tumors against the breakwall,
no channel to light.

        I was lost in anesthesia between
        the red sugar night & the golden
        city of waking.

In the history of my uterus, there has been only one area rug.
the bordering couch, bordering plant, the framed frame.

I used to believe:
        there are long red corridors & polished
wooden floors in the rooms of your uterus,

in the uterus of her & her, that she & she
        get up in the morning & notice the trees
        & the reflection of light on the lake is stunningly
        calming for the she's & the stillness isn't death but another
        kind of life:

        I was wrong.

                        x   x   x

In the hospital/

        I can't think my supernatural thoughts/
leap tall buildings/can't put together a sentence/can't
speak it—& you know that's everything—

        I see my beautiful husband's
face & can't reach for him—

I wonder about the dying, how people confess their sins to them
as a courageous act/the whole time the dying person thinking:
        get this person out of here

                        x   x   x

What would *you* bring back from the surgeon's table?

Don't bore me with what you've read—

    your latest frozen sea, your house on fire—
    I've got my hands full right here.

    I want to know what the blood knows
    how the red sugar says: stay or go/
    how to snap back my wrist/
                like a switchblade/
    how to know if ten years from now the people I love will turn
into someone else, if all this living is worth it/how to jack ahead/
& get to the sweet pulp of it/stop thinking I don't know
what I know, how to read the tea leaves;
    what my birth father's life was like/why he won't claim
me, I want lineage, serum, all the thick gooey answers:
stock & strain; pedigree;
              —I said,
    take everything out—all my insides—
they don't relate to anything anyway;

                      x   x   x

Days before my father died, I went to set the record straight/
crazy idea/him waving his hand in front of me saying/
it's not important/it's not important—then,
I think I know who you are by now—the most beautiful
words for me, words so sheer I slid my hands right through them.
When light left & the big wall came,

I was in my apartment, walking my own brutal planet
of knives & tightropes without a plan for love.

When I got to the hospital/I saw his body/so empty
without him/
      & it was no outer space adventure/
      nothing mystical: one hand
      on the door, then gone

               X   X   X

& my body now, coming apart—

      think storeroom & honeycomb,
      studio apartment, tastefully decorated:

            Look, I'm building a house
            from scratch, don't talk to me
            about family, about sweet—

            family history, anyone
            in your family have cancer?

            I slashed the surgeon's form
            with a rough X—scrawled: ADOPTED
            across it in 4-inch letters—

I said, *Take everything out*

            not holymarymotherofgod
            blahblah at the hour

of our uterus, teach me how
to love if I can't be a mother
oh god oh blah precious mother

x   x   x

Some days the world demands a dress of me—

something to parade around in—

& some days I do too:

       inside out, I'm stitched with hair/
       beaded with eyes/all my seeds
       arranged for you/

       but lately since I died inside—
       (fuck the bloody show)
       I'll keep my body mine.

~~*Postscript to the babies that never were:~~
~~I carry your outline on the inside of my eye=~~
~~lids, I carry your blood in my eye~~

x   x   x

Outside is nothing, nothing, nothing. I will construct
three leaning crosses for my uterus:
one for the useless waiting boat,
one for the promised city with its shimmering lake,
one for everything that's not coming.

Then I'll burn it all down.

x   x   x

Procreate this:

Who is the woman after flight?

she's the night/

coming into view:

x   x   x

A Necessary Waist: Plath Grows Thinner Reading Stein

. . . what is the current that presents a long line
and a necessary waist
— Gertrude Stein

1. The outside pressing in like a red lake,

   causing a narrowing of her.

   Will there be room for everything/everyone inside?

2. Because also inside her: a rope and a map:

   rope of intestines, marking the equator of her

   like the belt of a shirtwaist dress,

   map of her mother's face,

   every line and malignant flap of skin.

3. A recording like a tapeworm: *do not return to this*

   and

   this is everything, everything

   you don't want to be.

Dreaming Door

for Don

You brought donuts in the morning of our first days and
we watched the great rivers through my South Side windows/everything
swelling, we ate in the turquoise kitchen and opened the dreaming door:
our Pittsburgh rolling by on the coal barges, the P&LE carting steel
to the still-rising cities of the West, a couple speedboats
running the dirty summer Monongahela,
you on your way to work. I said *no one's ever*
been this nice to me as I walked you the 52 steps down
from my third floor apartment, you tilted your head,
looking at me in a way I'd never seen:
like I was the most sublime person,
your blue eyes seeming truly puzzled:
I haven't even started to love you yet,
and at the door the world barreling through—
this time with gifts, fierce fires,
and planets of luck.

The Punch

My father at thirty
knows the bend over & take it,
but he also knows the flipped switch,
the moment of recalcitrance, when the burn
turns to fire, when the body's magma rises
up, comes out the mouth in a full-blown

motherfucker, when the fist swings high
in its 60-degree orbit to an uppercut.
130 lbs, all frame, he knows the full 90
into a roundhouse slam, then the walking
away, not broken, but changed.
My father's geometry is one body

up against the wall with trouble
on your hands, but less trouble than
if you turned your back, & sometimes
anger is the only right language.
His punches swing clean like a pendulum
into his boss's big-knob head & barrel-chest:

Beatty, get over here and re-do this,
you really fucked this up—
& my father knows he did a fine job,
that this is the language of breaking a man down
until he doesn't fight anymore, because
my father is mouthy, he's union,

Steelworkers Local #1272,
he has opinions about hours & working conditions,
the air they're breathing. When his boss

calls him out, his head lifts to a glare—
he walks slowly over & delivers an uppercut
to the jaw, with a trajectory that leads

from ground to body in a geometry so sweet
you can figure distance, velocity, & angle
to conjure the exact position of the bodies
when the blows are struck, ciphering
through mathematical model the reason
2 grown men/bodies 10 inches apart/

round their fists up & swing a parabola
from this cement floor to this corrugated wall/
figuring in the percentages: rage infused
by union-management history/X the cost
of one man's life in this rust town,
city of steelworkers who built the country/

adding: 2 daughters/the price of 1 man's
dignity & a life of work—1 roundhouse
punch/the backswing casting off blood
in a spatter on the wall of the mill, decking
the boss in a circle of steelworkers cheering:
red on grey a siren bleating: /violation/

so that the investigator will find
an overlay on the corrugated steel:
blood, spatter over spatter.

Love Poem w/Strat

My baby's got a solid-body
guitar, rocks it hard like dinosaurs
eating cars, plays it dirty like worlds
exploding, like Stevie Ray's battered strat,
Badlands sticker on the back, he's got a fever
for the steamroller, like Hendrix on Voodoo Child,
like Jeff Beck avalanching notes into air/
my baby's a gunslinger, plays
his guitar rock-hard—
he likes it old-style, he likes it Muddy,
likes it Elmore James, bends it crazy
on his '62 reissue arctic white strat
& his head rolls back/
to that precise pain, that one note screaming,
his mouth twisted open & the light crossing
his face like a freight train passing—
my baby's a gunslinger, plays
his guitar rock-hard—
he likes it Freddie King/whole body vibrato/
likes it Howlin Wolf, my baby plays it
strings-against-the-mic-stand dirty/twists
the body to the Hubert Sumlin script/screams
through his Fender vibro-king—he's
got a hard-on for traditional, fuck
special effects, fuck overplay/he's got love
for his whammy bar, got love
for his double cutaway fins, jams
his headstock into the air, rips a hole
in the sky with his song

Daughter of Blue Lake

Before I was born, I was a star
over Blue Lake, I was alive before
I was alive, hanging over Blue Lake
in the most romantic of ways—
I stayed until my name was called
and lived today—

          —my place now here,
sitting at your hospital bed watching
you die, I'm reading *Swimming to Antarctica*,
feeling that's how impossible it is
to lose you and waiting for the morphine
to take you and the sky carry you,
not knowing if you can hear,
telling everything I ever wanted
you to know:

Thank you for naming me, I say.
(When my parents picked me out
you told them what to call me)
I like my name, I say, and with eyes
closed you say, *You're welcome.*
I named you before you were born—

        and I'm stroking your hand as
        whatever holds things together
        lets loose, and beyond the field
        of this moment, we fly—

        I see you back then: gatekeeper
        of the other world, saying,
        here, this way, here she is,

delivering me from the shimmering
to the turbulence of the known world,
saying: *protect her, care for her*

In the hospital bed,
you never open your eyes
and in the body letting go, you usher me again
to this washing and grooming where
the waves and fault lines of the day take over—
this way/ over here/ no matter—
you are flying to your own open book,
your dead brother waiting for you in the car.

from *the switching/yard*

Visitation at Gogama

No shirt, was drying his long hair
with a towel and staring at the train,
he looked about 30.
I saw my birth father young and alive,
he stepped out of a brown house with a white
sign on the side: WILD BILL (his nickname)
in big block letters. I saw him the way he was
before he made me—
beautiful and astonishing in his maleness.
I tell you this is my family tree—no
noble phrases, no graveyards on the hill,
just visitations. Now pieces of discarded track,
explosion of purple wildflowers along the side,
solid wall of rock 5 ft from the train,
then a river/bridge/floating leaves
that look like giant lily pads—is that possible?
We're approaching the town of Gogama,
Ontario—small railroad town erased
by the diesel engine. There's a bar called
"Restaurant/Tavern" and a meat market
called "Meat Market" and a motel called
"Motel"—no other names.
In this place of no-naming or maybe
first-naming, I decide I'll call myself "bastard"—
it's plain and accurate, you can count on it.
We approach a signal, a woman in a
black tank top with killer arms slouches
in a grey Buick Century at the crossing
in a modified gangster lean. I decide
I love her, call her free.

California Corridor

On the San Joaquin Line
between Modesto & Merced,
past the arroyos, past the fruit trees
in rows, rows—hands of the farm workers/
beauty always with blood behind it,
nothing free. The holding tank
& the drainage ditch, the cast-off trucks
of the workers, woman & child wait
for the angels of bread to swoop down
& bring the night with them, covering
her & her baby, feeding them, saying
sleep, sleep. This day, California is a wide,
wide lover—sweet & slightly off-key
in its song. Wacky & loose, the train rumbles
through Richmond, Martinez, ocean
on the left, gang tags on the right beside
the paper mills, refineries,
the brown, brown hills—
then explosion of jacaranda (red flower!)
more mounds of brown, beautiful
red, a young couple playing cards
across the aisle: does she know the way
he looks at her is what people spend lives
looking for?
They're laughing/curling into
each other—he in his little skid hat/she's in a
striped tee—this kind of desire the most
radiant—from the body outward—
No way to be in CA & not feel *frontier*—
so many suffering drought/poverty/
only the hills outlast us—

How to have body/space/land of the mind/
knowing the ravaged?
Be awake in it,
one rail tie at a time.
I want to be in the open—
Out here, the land grows wild hair on the side
of the tracks the way a dead man grows his—
dry, stickly—so stray—going to a place no one
knows. Mountains are the only salvation—
windmills on the left, "Golden West" train
on the right, truck junkyard:
You left your soul in LA, the guy across
the aisle says to his friend.
Then why does he look so alive?
I was here, I was loved. Were you?
We go through Pittsburg, CA—factories shut
down here, too—where I met Wild Bill.
Blue blue cerulean next to brown dead hills—
otherworldly with the windmills—
standing water, huge pallets for transport &
we are riding through a feeling—suspension—
Nothing, nothing can be done right now/
we are free.

      Then all aboard in Antioch:
a skate punk kickflips his board
& sits down, hoodie w/skull & hat back-
wards, I love him for his pose, brilliantly
indestructible.

My Mother Was a Dress

For years I was wearing her,
she was cotton, her neck a blue V
for her blue vagina that birthed 6 babies.
She had a vanilla string around
her waist even though she was hooker-red
at heart, like me.

I wore her for two years, along with
a sister dress of deep cherry.
When I went to meet her the first time
at Catholic Social Services, I wore the cherry
and she wore the blue vagina.

We thought that genetics had made us
go to Joseph P. Hornes to buy the V,
but decided we both lived
near the bloodless dept. store.
After that, I took her off,
stopped wearing her,
didn't want her touching
my body anymore.

I prefer to think it's all animal—
the way the V opens my neck to predators,
the way she scissored her legs open
to my father's cock.
The way the dress hugs my hips
then falls,
just like she said she hugged me once—
before falling away, switching
me out for sale.

Sister as Moving Object

my sister is moving in me again
with her long   arms and legs

moving to tell me   she's still here
inside my body   along with fireballs

free-roaming breath   some days she's a tanker truck
magnetic   gleaming down my highways

some days   an ocean liner   splitting
the dark waters   today   my sister's particular beauty

rocks the house   to 1965   wearing pink-pink-
caked-on lipstick   tight pants   teased-up-

Ann-Margaret hair   could've been anyone's
sister and was   adopted from another place

she raised me up   taught me   the necessary things:
how to mix   water with bourbon   in the picture-frame bar

how to mix   the real and the unreal   and make it glisten
sea of submerged heartache   great blanket of sea:

seamount   *sweptback*   *from the guyot to the springboard*
sluice   *railbed*   *heart of copper field*

nightshade   when she hid her arsonist boyfriend
in the basement closet   (when the cops came looking for him)

she taught me the power of a lie: *no, I haven't seen him*
no, not since yesterday   she taught me to be visible   then follow

the circle down: *ball bearings*   *axehandles*
fields of snakes   hot spur of escape   when she ran downstairs

to tip him off: *now! through the backyards*
they won't look there   she gave and gave   early lessons in desire

her and her dark-haired muscle boy   on the rock
behind the shopping center   me the lookout   air thick

with everything coming   his thin teeshirt   i watched their mouths:
|torrential| everything i wanted   moving through them

today I name the lasting roads: *artery*   *toll road*   *road of disguise*
she taught me imprisonment   not being a rat:

I took to the heat   like a dog to an electric fence   don't go past
the edge of the yard   2 girls blank from no beginnings   in combat

so tall   the only way to beat her   was to scissor her
between my thick legs   and squeeze

tonight   the house humming   her particular beauty:
lack of compromise   she grabbed the nail scissors   stabbed me:

sea of the head thrown back   she, later   dancing to loud music
said: *do it like this, don't listen*   *to what they tell you*

sea we never shared   blood sea

Three Faces and All These Fallen Gods

I'm surrounded by fallen gods in mosaic,
one with his shield battling a tiger and losing,

another with three heads: man/woman/girl rising
from a green vase in a bong-like cloud—just like my childhood—

The third with the god in exile, just him and his blunted sword
watching for the coming redemption (not pictured).

I'm in Tre Visi, 3 blocks from the Manitoba Hall of Fame
and my father's picture. It's all too much, the Canadians

are aesthetes, and I'm sure my birth father will walk in—
I'm reading James Allen Hall's poetry so as not to appear lonely,

but looking pitiful instead. I like the way he transgresses
the ugly with the tender. The brutality reminds me

of an article I read in Vanity Fair where this bank robber
visits his ex and sticks a .44 up her twat and how

I got turned on by that, but could never tell anyone—
who could I tell? How he would move the gun around inside her,

say things like, Is this too cold? Do you want me, instead?
I thought—how unusual to find a man who'll do that—

cross a hard line and whisper at the same time,
and the opera playing is Puccini's Tosca,

the waiters meeting my every need and I am filled
with magical thinking: my father has certainly eaten here,

his DNA here, I am in his seat in Winnipeg with three faces
and all these fallen gods/sinking into the *tre visi*:

three faces of longing, loss and desire—
wanting him to walk in, say, *I've been looking for you.*

Younger, I spent too many years wishing men
would say something hotter than I could think of—they never did.

Because really, I just want to be relieved of making it all up—
let *them* run it hard and right for a change.

If they could sell their body blazing with a gun, I'd buy it—
instead I eat my stracciatella and farfalle pretending

a reason to be here—I eat spicy sausage and the wanting
that keeps me in this seat, watching the door,

thinking, *yes, it's too cold—*
now, turn it a little.

Delicious

I'm looking for clothes to put my body in. At the family gathering, my sisters-in-law
wear sundresses & strappy sandals, which are lovely, & it's sunny out, but the Kenneth
Cole men's shirt I got on sale seems out of place, like the way I need to wear a lot of
metal that can double as weapons if needed & ever since I cut off all my hair years ago
to avoid being mistaken for a woman who wants a man in Dockers, I search websites for
men's shoes & shirts to fit, stores for men with elegant small feet, who I imagine to be
my cosmic brothers, then one sister-in-law talks about the new baby, the new baby, so I
switch to the men's talk about the new Camaro, the new Camaro, & the NFL's jacked-up
penalties on hitting, but always swing back to the women, who have a watery way
about them I love, who are talking about the zesty seasoning for the bean salad, which is,
in fact, delicious.

Top-10 List

Yes, that's the world—full of spears,
faceplates, iron stars.
       —Diane Glancy, The West Pole

When I taught in maximum,
the inmates turned in stories of rape & torture
with hoods, binding, cutting, maiming—

then they would hit on me. I told them
their language didn't hold up on the page.
They were brutal, like Viggo in Eastern Promises,

like tattooed Sean in Mystic River, like all my
ex-boyfriends. I know the world is full of spears,
faceplates, iron stars. Some days

as bad as Christian Bale in Terminator Salvation.
Some days I'm oceanic in my ambivalence/
lost in the big cosmic bath

where grief & ecstasy meet.
My friend Aaron says people are basically bad,
will stick you with a switchblade

at first chance. I say people are good,
because I can't continue any other way.
We argue our list of hot men:

His #1: Daniel Craig/mine: Viggo Mortensen.
Sub-categories: best body/
best underarms/forearms/

best shirtless.
We both love Lenny Kravitz, Sean Penn,
Denzel. Even after all the bad movies,

Aaron still wants to nail Brad Pitt.
My therapist started giving me quotes
from Philip Roth novels, but I couldn't

face those either: too bleak.
Aaron's hot for Anderson Cooper
& Colin Farrell—

while I like Ryan Gosling.
When I look at life straight on,
I'm Pacino in *Scarface*

(the balcony scene with the AK-47)
The bloody header into the pool,
my heart an iron star.

I have my spears: I'm jealous, vain,
I'm Ryan Phillippe in *Cruel Intentions*.
My faceplate:

I'm Joaquin Phoenix (wannabe-rapper/
post-rehab/eccentric & mumbling on Letterman)
I need tinted glasses to even go outside.

Youngest Known Savior

They talk in that *natural* way   shortcuts like: *got it*
or   *second shelf/left side*   and she thinks:

oh my god, they talk alike   her cousins
all have long eyelashes   [each one the same

black lash, naturally curled]   *She feels like she's falling*
deeper into alone   She goes   into the bedroom

with the pink sleeping thing   [baby]
she hates it   for how it lies there   how it

didn't have to   do anything   to get those same eyelashes
[white crib, ruffles]   *Only a 3 foot drop,*

she thinks   Later she tells them   [trying to approximate
their truncated speech]:   *She fell out of the crib*

and I put her back   [afterwards, in the bathroom,
she uses her cousin's eyelash curler]   How could she

learn their careful walk   the way they   move their heads
slight/left   She is 10   one of the youngest known

saviors   it's better now   Before today,
it was so tedious: *blood is blood*   and

she was never   one of them   [that was
before today]   before she learned   the language

Reading Wanda Coleman on the California Zephyr

Her sweet bebop a backdrop to floating white silos
out the window, hoodoo ghosts on the Osceola stop.
Pass an old car graveyard, then an orchard, dirt road/
black cow/black cow/how do we get around?
So much country, how do we even know where to go?
4:30 AM bathroom break/I peek down the narrow train,
a man's black shoe sticking out of a sleeper, all
the train murders in movies. In the bathroom, the handle
jiggles hard, hard—he's there. I wait/it stops/
look outside, the shoe is gone! I run back to Coleman:
traveling the backside of the underground/stranded
where the cul-de-sac crosses/the dead end.
Danger/anonymity, each little town's the same
from the train: road/signal/bar/car dealer
and earlier today a man and woman trip out of
the Triangle Bar, she's jerking her elbow from his hand,
they're fighting in Ottumwa on Saturday, 7.18.08
the California Zephyr watching. A woman lost
in the cracks in the big beautiful hole of America.
I'm sending a message to myself and the woman
from the bar—Coleman says *slavery's been dead nigh*
a century/or more but i carry my chain everywhere.
We're coming out of nowhere into the next nowhere.
Fog. whistle. banging. trees.
Houses in water up to picture windows,
garages left open, stains show levels 10 feet down,
still nowhere for the water to go after Midwest floods.
The attendant speaks as if from script:
Ladies and gentlemen:
you'll see a lot of standing water
on the right side of the train.

You'll see that some white pelicans
have made this their new home.
What used to be farmland is now a lake . . .
Sandbags stacked to hold the Mississippi, rail ties litter
tracks like fat sticks—where are the people?
Over the brown gargantuan
Mississippi into Iowa, over the timber trestle,
I think of the dead workers who made this, then look
at the swirling below, so alive.
The woman in the dining car:
This is America the beautiful.
I'm *a romantic,* she says.
Big logs of cars, tankers topped by green and yellow
lights that look like they're sitting on top of them
but really miles off—so many things miles off:
my husband at home with his kindness—
Time is alive and dead: the small red farmhouse,
aluminum silo, the narrow green sign.
Derrick in the distance, poking down
into ground like a crow.
Scaffolds of electrical poles like Darth Vader heads:
outcroppings, outjuttings, as if something couldn't
wait another moment to spring into the above-ground world.
Why is there only 1 tree, then 1 tree?
So much about edges out here—fenceline,
trackline, berm, the footpath by the berm,
fieldlines with road in-between. demarcation.
It names us.
Past/present, where we walk, where grass meets dirt/
where we end up.
A man is getting his mail, cornfields cornfields,

islands of trees mid-field, house in the distance.
Retired railcars in the town of Creston with a plaque.
Iowa needs some Wanda Coleman, someone who's
not afraid to say it hard. Soon the hills mound up
as we get closer to the Continental Divide—still
three hundred miles away, but the ground starting to shape differently.
So much under us unsaid.
This train makes me think of my birth father,
the smooth glide through nowhere,
alive in Boston, how I walk around in his nothingness.
How I look like him but don't know him.
I've always loved the foothills and the low brush—
Out the window, the ground sloping and rising,
I don't want to miss anything.
Why has he come to me now
on this train in the middle of my life?
I have a picture of his face, but I claim his body, too—
his 3 Stanley cups, the fight in him that's in me,
I need to walk the ground he walked, I want to see his home—
The feeling of space but something's coming:
a train right next to us whooshing in the other direction
single house with a light on.

The Switching/Yard

2 giant sleeping cranes, nothing as lonely as
a crane not working: relic with its head bowed
in the brokenness of a highway dream.
Crossbar signal/arm over the road with
red light eyes: we're coming.
Rolling out of Toronto with a derailment in Capreol—
14 cars off the track, but we're headed into it,
I'm riding the dirt line to Winnipeg,
where my birth father is deeper than the Assiniboine and
wider than the Red River Valley, he's
the whole province of Manitoba.
Lines of indigenous pines otherworldly now
because this is my country, I'm the indigenous one,

ghost explorer returning, looking for blood.
Moving again, just crossed the highway
outside of Wahago. 11:30 PM and the sky's
blue-dark with the trees going back to their night souls—
Is anyone else on this train tonight looking for ghosts?
From this 3×4 window I see underpass/
underpass/deserted road/so close to hillsides
we are inside the land.
Industrial construction yard, lines and lines of tracks—
The VIA Rail steward:
If you look here, you'll find the train #====
here's the name of each car.
Mine is *111 Bliss.*

Riding north of Thunder Bay to Winnipeg,
past the green green of Saskatchewan

to the prairies of Manitoba, nothing
but fields of dirtgrass for miles.
My father's father was here—and in some piece of dirt,
some line of crossing, the wind will whip up
into the Manitoba field-long clouds where
the Red River meets the union hall,
where miners and machinists said, here.
Here, where a switch can be made out of a willow,
where a switch can rise from dirt.
If I can stand in the crosscut of bodies that made my father,
that grew him hard into a crosschecking fighter,

I will have found blood.
There is no peace like the road at night,
until the whistle spills its fat long blare—
must be coming up on a town.
Tree branches hit the side of the train, a band
of light coats the trees in the distance in
the secret life of quonset hut/quonset hut/
all this industry and dreaming, people's lives
on these dark patches of land—are they up late
worrying about losing?
Their job, their minds, their families?
We are all so
separate with the same lives.

The train shaking me home to no father I know:
right wing for the Hornets/Maple Leafs/Rangers—
—his steps, my steps.
I can't see him/hear him/touch him

but I can walk the ground, step hard:
Was there a white frame house?
A woman, your mother, washing clothes
by the Red River? Are these the overalls
touched by your skin? The ground you walked
then two bodies slammed together
one night in Pittsburgh and I was made,
and in the making the blood ran?
Who made your green piercing eyes
that bore through me with aliveness/

In this ghost land,
lights show up in trees,
a band of light in the sky, a different look
every 20 yards, the change of it all.
House on the hill with 5 lights on, the kind
of house that always has porch lights burning—
there's a steadiness out here that I love,
a regularity I don't know. Sudden rise of land
and a highway tunnel. Sign: *Megalots*—160 *ft deep*
and city lampposts sprout like alien antennae.
The train stopping now, 3 cars unhitched—
left in the yard for pickup.
Where is that one sweep of wind where

I'll find the switching/yard: this train and that,
those who made you, and, in that distant
but bloody kingdom way—me,
so I can stand and say, here.
Here where Ukranian immigrants set their stake:

where the prairie met the working stiff
and you were born. Shut up in this
compartment, I am the small ghost—
light shines in the window from a signal,
shooting the whole traincar bloody red.
Tomorrow in the open I will be legion—
you will see me bleeding from every pore,
a woman in the switching/yard.

The Hit Man

I'd see him driving around, tanned
in his red truck with young stud helpers,
sometimes in the yards, teeshirt in his back pocket.
His name was Jelly, he came in every night at 6,
freshly shaved & cologned with Polo
after his landscaping gig, stood at the bar,
one foot on the brass rail, one on the floor.
In his 40's but solid: a short, fireplug of a man,
he'd talk trash for hours in his odd,
high-pitched voice & bellow in strangled,
spitted spurts—narrgghh!— repeating bits
of dialogue from his friend & drunk girlfriend:
. . . and the guy walked like a poodle!
or . . . she said, keep the fuckin money!
Did you hear that?—keep the fuckin money!
Everyone knew he had hurt people:
he was a closer, did what was needed.
But from the side, he was an Italian god,
his bulbous nose red from drinking
& the sun—his graying hair in waves
almost to his shoulders with a close-cut beard.
I'd bring out his food, he'd slip me a $20,
even though the bartender ran the tab—
he'd grab my cheeks & say, look at that face—
whadyu doin in this dump? I'd say, workin—
& he'd laugh. One night in late July,
the Pitt Panthers playing Marquette—
he had one eye on the corner TV,
but knew everything going on in the bar.
I walked up to him & asked:
Can you get me a gun?
He didn't look at me, didn't flinch,

lifted his Chivas on the rocks, said,
Whatdyu need a fuckin gun for?
To kill my boyfriend, I said.
He broke character, turned & looked at me,
bore a hole through me, bullet-like,
for a long 5 seconds.
I stared back.
He turned back to the game & laughed loudly.
No, he said quietly.
Why not? I said.
I ain't givin you a fuckin gun.
Why not?
Because you'd use it.
He tilted his head back, shook his hair,
running his fingers through it,
making a ponytail & then letting it loose.
He drank down the Chivas, his left pinky in the air—
perfectly manicured.
I'd had enough name-calling & arm grabbing &
wall punching & other women—
I reached down to find whatever gods I could—
& came up with him:
standing at the bar with his girlfriend Patty
until she couldn't walk from shots.
There is no one else, I thought,
no one who would help me.
That night, in the crashed-out summer of '85,
waiting for his bookie, his connection,
he wasn't free either.
We were brother & sister:
as noble as yours or yours—

Ghostdaddys

When I was a girl I was a boy
with black boots and holster and
a basketball hoop in the backyard.
My reach was endless, I was
birthed in a meteor shower and
all the stars knew my name.
Ever since, I've been on street corners
with gimcrack men you wouldn't want to know,
making myself a luminary.
I had this piece of paper—took years to get it:
the story before the story changed,
before the government got their hands on it.
I've been told _____.

My first father was a millionaire, his
name on my birth certificate/voice
on the phone/his lame-ass answer:
I didn't come inside her.
I was the small voice asking/
he was the hammer coming down,
shattering me into shooting stars.
I covered my bedroom ceiling
with planets, prayed for a meteor hit
to bury the house. My second father

was a hockey player who fucked
my mother when she was 20—
I drove to Boston to meet him, armed
with her picture, he didn't
remember her: *I was a professional*

athlete, he said, *there were a lot of women.*
His green eyes burned familiar,
and I thought he was a good man—then
two weeks later, he said no, he didn't
think he could be my father. I decided
I've come from a long line of cowards,
men who can only stand up if they're

fucking/flaccid after that.
Sometimes the earth moves in my dreams
with lies about my past. I was
bent on ruination: drugs for lunch
and dinner—with some dope in between.
My face the face of no/
father, unrecognizable/so why not?
I was the immaculate cum-shot,
I was the wildly surviving thing,
racing after ghostdaddys in dreams:
Dear father, whoever you are,

I hope the sex was ravenous,
with cross/checking, slashing/
I hope there were slats of light everywhere
to see my star on the other side.

Dear American Poetry,

I see you're publishing:
straightman/straightman/white white white how
nice.

Are you kidding me?
Best American Poetry, I'm bored to death—is anyone
alive out there?

Your sonnet is impotent,
and I
have a hard-on.

Here's your bloody sonnet:

       cŭnt cúnt/cŭnt cúnt/cŭnt cúnt/cŭnt cúnt/cŭnt cúnt/

       thĕ née/dlĕ dićk/thĕ neé/dlĕ dićk/thĕ née-/

American poetry, tell your mother
you'll be home late—
if anyone's out there waiting for you to lick them good,

it'll be a long night.
I was once fucked by an intellectual in iambic pentameter:
my hand was better, and more responsive.

your friend,
Jan Beatty

Drinking the Lizard King

God of the soft parade, mojo king and
poet of Venice, and second song
he started: *Wishful, sinful, our love is beau-*
ti-ful . . . stripped his shirt down to muscled
shoulders, threw it in the audience to bloody
screaming, slid into his sideways lizard-king
walk, unbuckled his belt, whiplashing
his leg with it/we all wanted to die
inside that slap/down to the neon/
and we knew there were two kinds of people
in the world: people who loved Jim Morrison
for pissing on the audience—and Republicans:
he copped a stance, waving his cock
like it was *the way, the truth, and the life,*
and it was—just to be covered in him—
we opened our mouths, and when the cops
rushed the Miami stage, he dropped to his knees,
his neon-green jockstrap glowing,
he grabbed his cock out and
swung it like a firehose as they dragged
him off—and we were baptized
in the water of the lizard king,
we were *stoned, immaculate.*
To be pissed on by the god Morrison
was like being fucked in a muscle car—
all cylinders firing full out
and nothing in the way.

Notes on a Nevada Flood

for Don

There's a mountain outside my window & a lake full
with glacial water & it's
flooding in my heart—chamber by chamber—
I'm a woman in the middle
of my life running backwards towards the center,
the master flood.
Piles of sandbags, holding back
the washing of the gone dreams.
So many things miles off—my husband at home
with his brilliant sweetness—
A mountain outside my window &
a dark blue lake full—
& close to here, on an old forest road,
a woman is walking to get her mail—
she will hear today that

————————————————,

& I'm thinking of her flowered dress & mountain
boots, her wondrous life on the edges—
Who will write her story, where does her life go—
all the lives above—the swirling below.
There's a mountain outside my window
but all I want:

the flood of heart in a closed room with you—
your arm flung sloppily across me,
hitting my face, your other hand playing guitar
in deep sleep.
Oh, wild dreaming one—if you were here,
what would you say?
That I'm swirling towards death in my own

eddying ideas?
No, you would say, *go to sleep, are you okay?*
(the only blessing I need tonight)
Goodnight to everyone alive—
Wherever I am, I'm filled with sediment:
with tough, dirty Pittsburgh
where the mountains of black rock &
half mills are carapaces.
Night coming now,
& the hills mounding up as we get closer
to the continental divide of you & I—of death—
No stopping the water:
almost pristine in the quiet.

notes

New Poems

"Asylum" refers to Roselia Asylum and Maternity Hospital, located in the Hill District of Pittsburgh where I was born and spent the first year of my life. It opened in 1891 and was staffed by the Sisters of Charity.

"The Secret Book and Record Store" refers to the store of that name on Wicklow Street in Dublin, Ireland.

"The World between Jim Morrison's Legs" references "18th and Speedway" in Venice Beach, California, where a mural of Morrison fills the alley. Its formal name is Morning Shot, painted by the artist Rip Cronk. In some circles, Morrison is regarded as a patron saint of the Westside, as Our Lady of Guadalupe is sometimes regarded as traditional muse for the Eastside. Morning Shot stands as storied mythology, recalling the 1965 meeting between Morrison and Ray Manzarek on the Venice boardwalk. Harold Perry is an iconic figure of the boardwalk. The John Carruthers guitar refers to a famous guitar builder for musicians like the Rolling Stones, The Doors, Bob Weir, Frank Zappa, Joni Mitchell, Merle Haggard, and many more. He owned a historic shop in Venice Beach, where he remained for thirty years.

"Dropping Blotter Acid at the Slag Dump" makes use of lines from the Observer Reporter, November 18, 1997.

"The Secret Book and Record Store" is for Tess Barry.

"Low-Rider" is for Aaron Smith.

"The Snapping" is for Judith Vollmer.

"Blue Rider" is for Nikki Pike.

"Against Suicide" is for Kayla Sargeson.

"Wedding Shoes" is for Don.

from Boneshaker

"Poetry Workshop at the Homeless Shelter" is dedicated to the residents of Wood Street Commons.

"Near the Foundling Home" refers to Roselia Foundling Home, a home for unwed mothers in Pittsburgh.

"My Father Teaches Me to Dream" is in the voice of R. T. Beatty.

"Cruising the Blue Belt" is for the beautiful world.

from Red Sugar

"Lip" is for Tamara DiPalma.

"Red Sugar" makes use of some phrases from *A Match to the Heart* by Gretel Ehrlich.

"The Phenomenology of Sex" is dedicated to Judith Vollmer.

"When Foucault Entered the Body" is for Aaron Smith.

"The Punch" is for Robert T. Beatty, who worked for J& L Steel in Pittsburgh, Steelworkers Local #1272, Southside Works.

"Love Poem w/Strat" makes use of lines from "The Stratocaster," an article by David Fricke, in which he quotes guitarist Joe Perry, *Rolling Stone*, issue 922, May 15, 2003.

"Daughter of Blue Lake" is in memory of Charlotte Thoma.

from The Switching / Yard

"Visitation at Gogama" was written on the VIA Rail Canadian from Toronto to Jasper.

"California Corridor" makes use of a phrase from *Imagine the Angels of Bread* by Martín Espada. It was written while riding the San Joaquin in Northern California.

"Sister as Moving Object" was written after reading the work of James Allen Hall and D. A. Powell.

"Top-10 List" is for Aaron Smith.

"Reading Wanda Coleman on the California Zephyr" was written on the California Zephyr from Pittsburgh to Denver while reading Coleman's *Ostinato Vamps* and *The Riot Inside Me: More Trials & Tremors*.

"The Switching/Yard" was written on the VIA Rail Canadian from Toronto to Jasper.

"Ghostdaddys" makes use of a phrase from "Chronic" by D. A. Powell.

"Drinking the Lizard King" is for Kayla Sargeson. "Drinking the Lizard King" loosely refers to the performance of Jim Morrison and the Doors on March 1, 1969, at the Dinner Key Auditorium in Coconut Grove, Florida, commonly known as "The Miami Incident." On March 5, the city of Miami issued a warrant for Morrison's arrest, after a complaint that was signed by an office boy who had gone to the show, and who happened to work for the state attorney. The Dade County State Attorney's Office issued a felony charge of lewd and lascivious behavior and five misdemeanors: two counts of indecent exposure, two for public profanity, one for public drunkenness. This was followed by *Rolling Stone* publishing the "Wanted in Dade County" cover photo of Morrison, with the article "Morrison's Penis Is Indecent." www.doors.com

acknowledgments

The author wishes to acknowledge the following journals in which some of these new poems first appeared, sometimes in earlier versions:

Academy of American Poets, Poem-a-Day ("The Kindness"); *Black Tongue Review* ("She Set Me Swimming"); *Cimarron Review* ("Low-Rider," "Dropping Blotter Acid at the Slag Dump"); *Court Green* ("Against Suicide," "Muscle Beach, Venice, 2013"); *5AM* ("Wedding Shoes"); *Florida Review* ("Abortion with Gun Barrel"); *Great River Review* ("The Snapping," "The Secret Book and Record Store"); *Narrative Northeast* ("Praise Blue," "Blue Rider"); *Paterson Literary Review* ("Inside the Cardinal," "Lake is a red pigment," "Taking Off, I Talk to the Dead"); *Pittsburgh Poetry Review* ("Surfing Cowboys," "The Boy from Hazard," "The World Between Jim Morrison's Legs"); *Pittsburgh Quarterly Online* ("I Knew I Wasn't Poor"); *Poetry* ("Asylum," "An eater, or swallowhole, is a reach of stream," "Stricken," "I Knew I Wasn't Poor").

"Youngest Known Savior" appeared in *Best American Poetry,* 2013.

Other poems in this collection have appeared in the following books:

Mad River, University of Pittsburgh Press, 1995.
Boneshaker, University of Pittsburgh Press, 2002.
Red Sugar, University of Pittsburgh Press, 2008.
The Switching/Yard, University of Pittsburgh Press, 2013.

I would like to express my appreciation to the Pittsburgh Foundation, the Pittsburgh Cultural Trust, the Howard Heinz Endowments, and the Laurel Foundation; the Creative Capital Foundation; Pennsylvania Council on the Arts; Brush Creek Ranch; Hedgebrook; Jentel; Leighton Studios, Banff, Alberta, Canada; the MacDowell Colony; Paterson Poetry Center; Ragdale; the Santa Fe Arts Institute; Split This Rock; Ucross; and the Platte River Whooping Crane Trust, James L. Grahl Research Center for fellowships and support that helped me to write these poems. Thanks to Carlow University for a sabbatical that enabled me the time and space to work. Special thanks to the wonderful staff at the University of Pittsburgh Press, especially Maria Sticco and David Baumann for above and beyond support and good-natured kindness; Alex Wolfe and Joel Coggins for editing and a cool cover.

So many people have helped me with these poems over the years, and I am indebted to all of them. I especially want to thank Ed Ochester for laser advice, stellar editing, and radical patience; my friend and partner in the wild land of poetry, Judith Vollmer, for unparalleled wolf-vision and traveling poems; Aaron Smith for continued friendship, the best relentless and dirty poems; Kayla Sargeson, the original wild Puff; Tess Barry, fierce Sagittarian, for unstoppable poems, and Thom for Blanco-tinis and their unflinching generosity; Nancy Kirkwood, bloodsister, for blue glasses and partly forthcoming nature; Lisa Alexander, adventurer, for compressed poems that are big and wide; Michael Wurster, poetry hero; All the Madwomen who are mad and they are many—you will rule the world; Gerry Rosella Boccella for unlimited heart and tender poems; Lucienne for wild spirit; Gayle Reed Carroll for her turning poems; Gail Langstroth for Eurythmy and wild leaping; Joan Bauer and Don for the Venice Beach residency; M. A. for bravery; Sheila Carter-Jones (Hammer); Jimmy Cvetic, Secret Society of Dog; the Carlow gang for monster support, especially Lou, Sigrid, Anne, Roberta, and Sarah; Allison Hedge Coke, psychic sister, for the esplanade burial; Colleen K. for big vision and fun; Gerry LaFemina for road-trip duende; Bounce for unflappable humor; Cosmic Donna from Surfing Cowboys; William Harry Harding for kind poem support; Maria Mazziotti Gillan for the dragon and red Mustang rides; Denise Duhamel for over-the-top coolness; Amanda Pope for one-of-a-kindness in L.A.; Dr. Robin for his big heart; Anne Rashid for Pigeon River; Emily Mohn-Slate and Daniela Buccilli for killer mentoring; Liane Ellison Norman for courage and exquisite poems; Lowell Britson, Zen master of Stinson Beach; Doug Powell for tea at Samovar; Sharon Hawkins for killer boots and talks; Brain Siewiorek for diggable hair; Michelle Stoner for Dennis and fearless poems; Natalie Diaz and Monique for the river ride; Marla for Pisces haircuts and trip/hop; Sarah Williams-Devereux for mad capers; Laurin Wolf for green and groovy interviews; Peter Oresick for *Iconosocope* and amazing spirit; Robin Behn for saying yes; RJ Gibson, original of originals; Kay Comini for loving the sentimental; Erin Figgins for super-tinted patience; Susan Sailer for fierce desire; M. L. Leibler for rock hard poems; Lovely Camilla at Marathon Car Rental in L.A.; Dr. G. for getting it; David Trinidad and Tony Trigilio for years of killer *Court Green*; Michelle and Lisa for fearsome sound engineering; Maggie Anderson for the tennis shoes; Tom Barber for fighting back; Jay Flory for great spirit; Judith Pond for Banff pizza; Stacey Waite for saying it; Marilyn Marsh Noll for extraordinary poems; Camille Norton still for election night in Stockton; Aiden Angle for his love of cymbals; Belinda Smith for great songs and the Nashville residency; Dr. K. for years of head help; Dorothy Holley for cheese and tomato sandwiches; Beatrice Vasser for courage; Tom and Barb for all the years; Anita Gevaudan Byerly for pool hall dancing; Eleanor Hooker, Clodagh Beresford Dunne, and Kathy D'Arcy for relentless energy and inspiring poems; Thomas McCarthy for unparalleled generosity and kindness; Afaa Michael Weaver for super cool and the next truck; Alicia Ostriker for tough, beautiful poems; James Allen Hall for dinner in Minneapolis and lunch in Pittsburgh; Bruce Weigl for going deep; Tam-o for the Ennis days; Michael Thomas for Meatpacking workshops; Rupa and Sagan for the future; Nancy Koerbel for carrying on; Sarah Browning for brave new work and opening the world; Dan, Camisha, Simone, and Tiana for Split This Rock love; Jessica Treat for integrity and never quitting; Nikki Pike and Shark for speaking in poems; Cynthia Hogue for the blue talisman; Joseph Bathanti for his big heart; Pat Bernarding for being there; Britt Horner for kindness and good talk; Anne Marie Macari for the Red Deer; Jerry Stern for Pittsburgh days; Extra thanks to Diane Glancy for naming the in-between; Richard Blanco for hard poems and biceps; Patricia Smith, world-changer; Rhoda Mills Sommer for more cool glasses and spirit; Remembering Wild Bill Ezinicki, crosschecker/blood carrier; Bob Patak, who lives in the rocks and wind; Wanda Coleman, wild and original poet; Ai, who took all the risks; Patricia Dobler who teaches us still; Charlotte Thoma, dream protector; Vee and Big Jim and the new 40 ft. guitar; R.T. Beatty, my father of fathers; and always and most for Don, my heart.